101
things to buy before you die

101
things to buy
before you die

Maggie Davis
Charlotte Williamson

RED ROCK PRESS NEW YORK

101 Things to Buy Before You Die
Maggie Davis and Charlotte Williamson

Red Rock Press, New York, NY
www.RedRockPress.com

ISBN 978 1 933176 24 6

Second edition

Copyright © 2006, 2007: New Holland Publishers (UK) Ltd
Copyright © 2006, 2007 in text: Maggie Davis and Charlotte Williamson

First published in 2006 by New Holland Publishers
London • Cape Town • Sydney • Auckland
www.newhollandpublishers.com

Davis, Maggie, 1975–
  101 things to buy before you die / by Maggie Davis and Charlotte
Williamson. -- 2nd ed.
       p. cm.
  Originally published: London : New Holland, 2006.
  ISBN 978-1-933176-24-6
  1. Shopping--Guidebooks. 2. Luxuries--Guidebooks. I. Williamson,
Charlotte, 1975- II. Title: III. Title.One hundred one things to buy
before you die. IV. Title: One hundred and one things to buy before you
die.
   TX335.D387 2008
   640.73--dc22

                              2008014215

Picture credits

With special thanks to Esther Adams, Olivia Bergin, Ruth Caven and Alfred Tong.

All images of products kindly supplied by the respective companies, except for those images credited below. Additional credits for
photographers and companies are also given: t=top, b=bottom, l=left, r=right, c=center

Front cover: Lulu Guinness bag, Lulu Guinness; Hermés Birkin bag, Rob Grieg; Cartier watch, Cartier; YSL lipstick, Rob Grieg; Manolo Blahnik
stiletto, Rob Grieg. Back cover: Bocca Marilyn Lips sofa, photo courtesy of Edra; Christian Louboutin stilettos, Rob Grieg. Front flap: Swarovski
chandelier, photographed by Andrea Ferrari; Leica MP camera, Leica. Back flap: Oliver Peoples sunglasses, Oliver Peoples.

Rob Grieg: 2, 3, 10, 16(t), 16(b), 19, 21, 26, 29, 34(t), 34(b), 35(t), 35(b), 36, 37(t), 37(bl), 37(br), 43(t), 43(b), 45(t), 45(b), 53, 57, 58, 60(l), 60(c), 60(r), 61(t),
62(t), 62(c), 62(b), 63(t), 63(b), 65, 66(t), 66(b), 67(t), 67(bl), 67(br), 68(t), 68(b), 69(t), 69(c), 69(b), 70(t), 70(b), 72, 73(l), 73(r), 74, 79(t), 79(b), 80, 87, 99,
106, 126, 127, 128, 131, 136(t), 136(b), 137, 140(t), 140(c), 140(b), 142, 144, 146(t), 146(b), 150(t), 150(c), 150(b), 151(t), 151(b), 152(t), 152(b)

Scooter, photo courtesy of Piaggio: 1, 159; Tom Dixon Ball Chandelier for Swarovski, photographed by Andrea Ferrari: 6; Goyard hand-painted monogram copyright © Goyard: 9; Kilgour suit, photo copyright © Sean Ellis: 13; Cadolle Bra, photo copyright © Louisa Parry: 17; Earnest Sewn Jeans / Xavier Brunet: 22;
Burberry Raincoat, photo copyright © Mario Testino: 30; Charvet Shirts, photo rights reserved (AMC): 31; Jim Thompson silk, photo copyright © Hans Fonk: 32,
33(tl), 33(bl), 33(r); Almas Caviar, photo courtesy of Cavier House & Prunier: 41, 42; Kopi Luwak Coffee, photo copyright © 1005 Todd Dalton & Edible Ltd: 49;
Gelato © Envision/Corbis: 51; Spice © Peter Adams/Zefa/Corbis: 54; Tea, photo copyright © John Rice Photography, www.johnricephoto.com: 55; Bed, photo
courtesy of Duxiana: 77; Barcelona chair, photocourtesy of The Aram Store: 82; Arne Jacobsen 3107 chair, photo courtesy of Twentytwentyone: 83 (tl);
Lounge Chair and Ottoman, design Charles and Ray Eames, 1956, photo: Hans Hanse: 83 (b); Chandelier Small Nest by Yves Béhar for Swarovski, photographed by Andrea Ferrari: 84; Coffee Tables, photos courtesy of Aram: 90(t), 90(b); Global Knife Block, photo courtesy of John Lewis: 97; Amish Quilt, photo
copyright © Lonely Planet Images / Richard I'Anson: 101; Jasper Morrison Cappellini Elan sofa, photo courtesy of SCP Ltd: 104 (t); Antonio Citterio Charles sofa,
photo courtesy of B&B Italia: 104(b); Bocca Marylin Lips sofa, photo courtesy of Edra: 105; Tablecloths, photo courtesy of Busatti: 107; Portuguese Tiles, photo
courtesy of www.portugal2u.com (Oscar Amara): 109; Legendary Lesotho Diamond, photo courtesy of Harry Winston / © Hans Gissinger 2004: 116; Gems ©
Royalty-free/Corbis: 117; Mikimoto Pearls, photo courtesy of Mikimoto: 120; Breitling Bentley 6.75, photo courtesy of Watches of Switzerland: 123; Madova
Gloves, s.r.l by Andrea Donnini: 135; Louis Vuitton Luggage, photo copyright © Antoine Jarrier: 138 (t); Manolo Blahnik stiletto, photo courtesy of Peartree:
145; Aston Martin, photo courtesy of Aston Martin: 153, 156; Apache Skis, photo courtesy of Snow and Rock (0845 1000 1000, www.snowandrock.com):
158; Tennis racquet courtesy of Babolat Vs: 160.

Contents

Introduction

Since we published the first edition of *101 Things to Buy Before You Die*, much has changed in the world of consumerism. Most notably, a backlash against that seemingly innocuous adjective "fast:" fast food, fast travel, and—to the raised eyebrows of the fashion world—fast fashion. The reason behind this consumer U-turn is simple: thanks to the relentless bombardment of advertising, not to say the intrinsic belief that "we're worth it," we're buying *way* too much stuff, and in the process producing more waste than is sustainable in the long term. The solution isn't merely to go green; rather, it is to consume less.

This may sound strange, especially coming from a shopping guide, but consuming less—and, ergo, the best—has always been our guiding principle. Buying half a dozen dresses at $50 a throw is a false economy: they might look—and indeed feel—great on the first wearing, but what of the fifth, the sixth? Heck, will they even make it that long? On the other hand, the right designer LBD will last for years, decades, even generations; the same can be said for more practical products such as the right toaster or sofa—just as disposable as those cheap frocks, but need this be the case?

In our updated edition we prove you can buy less by buying judiciously. We have honed in on items that have durability: tried-and-tested classics that offer true value for money; investment pieces that stand the test of time. And with products that won't last a lifetime—coffee beans, say, or stationery—we've concentrated on finding products with a strong artisan tradition and, where possible, a Fairtrade policy.

For both of us, shopping is an unashamed passion. As lifestyle journalists, we're forever being asked to track down the top products available on the market. We're the kind of girls who obsessively jot down tidbits of shopping information every time we hear them, whether it's the best paint color for a front door, wrinkle-reducers that actually work or chocolate that's good enough to make your toes curl with happiness. We've gone bananas over many things… such as the perfect mattress for a good night's sleep. In such weary times, the perfect mattress is pretty crucial.

Hence this book. *101 Things to Buy Before You Die* is a collection of the very best in food, fashion, furniture and fun. Up to a point, our guide is subjective. We had one important rule: a bona fide justification for each of our choices. So we've asked specialist buyers and those in the know for their suggestions: some are spectacular and, of course, super-expensive; others surprisingly reasonable—proof that money doesn't always buy the best. Many of the items have been selected because of their cult status; others are more about craftsmanship or heritage. Each product includes a gorgeous illustration to inspire and whet the appetite further, plus two alternatives that are often more affordable. More importantly, each choice is unbiased—no company has paid to be in this guide.

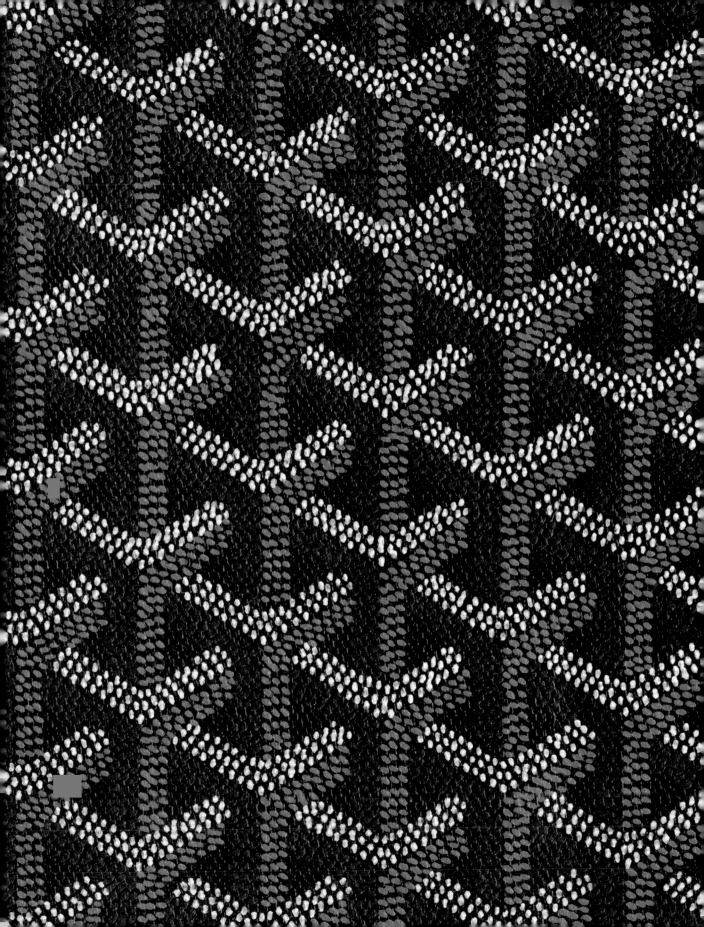

Between us we've done a *lot* of shopping and much of it has been done abroad. As the Victorians demonstrated so gloriously on their Grand Tours, when they picked up bespoke marbled stationery in Florence and heavenly fragrances in Paris, a canny shopper knows it's crucial to go global to get the best deals. But if you don't have the time to source your spices in Jodphur, that's where the internet comes in handy: global shopping at the click of a button.

The book is divided into seven sections for easy reference: Clothes, Food & drink, Health & beauty, Home, Jewelry, Shoes & accessories, and Leisure. The prices are in dollars and sometimes also in the currency of the country of origin of the item, and in most cases they are rounded off to the nearest figure. To help further, we've included invaluable advice on shopping for certain purchases—what to look for when buying a diamond, for instance, or how a good glass of champagne should taste—plus tips on haggling and etiquette in a souk.

Everyone shops. Not everyone *likes* to shop, but they need to. Yet if done properly, even the most mundane of shopping can be fun; a stick-in-the-mud retrograde man could enjoy bartering in a bazaar or browsing the gorgeous calfskin luggage at Hermès in Paris. If you know what you're looking for—and where to look—shopping becomes hassle-free. You may not agree with our choices, but we hope you'll agree with our reasoning and start buying better stuff. If nothing else, *101 Things to Buy Before You Die* will make you a more discerning shopper.

Maggie Davis and Charlotte Williamson

Clothes

"The finest clothing made is a person's, skin, but, of course society demands something more than this."

Mark Twain, 1835–1910

Bespoke suit

Henry Poole

Where?
15 Savile Row, London W1 • Poole tailors visit over 10 U.S. cities; check website for places and times: www.henrypoole.com

How much?
From £2,400/$4,350

There's no more grown-up, pivotal purchase a man can make than a handmade bespoke suit. The ultimate expression of power, professionalism, and gentlemanliness, it is to men what the perfect little black dress is to women—a wardrobe staple that is timeless, effortless and easy. From the streets of Milan to Paris and London, Europe has a rich heritage of bespoke tailoring, but nowhere has quite the same reputation as London's Savile Row, the established home of the bespoke suit. But where do you go for the ultimate? It's tough to pinpoint the absolute best—there are now around 10 genuine bespoke tailors on Savile Row—but Henry Poole is certainly one of the most respected.

Henry Poole

The company, which celebrated its 200th anniversary in 2006, has been making bespoke suits for royalty ever since Edward VII (a renowned arbiter of taste) granted the company a royal warrant in the early 20th century. The process is thorough and meticulous: it takes at least three appointments to get the ideal suit. The tailor starts by taking your measurements to make a pattern for the body. This is finely tuned at the second fitting, where the tailor checks details, such as the distance between the back collar and the shoulders as well as the trouser break on the shoes. At the third fitting, final details and adjustments are made. The end result is slick, smart, and utterly sophisticated, but also something that fits like a second skin. As Henry Poole's Managing Director, Simon Cundey, points out: "The aim is to feel like you're not wearing a suit at all."

Henry Poole showroom

KILGOUR

Kilgour

Where? 8 Savile Row, London W1 • Website calendar lists nine tape measure U.S. cities: www.8savilerow.com

How much? From £2,450/$3,600

Founded in 1882, Kilgour, a brand that has dressed the likes of Fred Astaire, Cary Grant and, more recently, Hugh Grant and Bryan Ferry, has glided smoothly into the 21st century. In 2004, this Savile Row shop was refurbished, becoming a modern, minimalist space in which the suits hang like objets d'art, but the traditional tailoring methods remain the same. Every element of a Kilgour suit is bespoke, from cutting the cloth to the fine art of finishing. It's one of the last establishments in Savile Row that preserves the one tailor, one garment system; it takes one tailor at least 80 hours to complete a single suit.

HUNTSMAN

Where? 11 Savile Row, London W1 • 00 44 207 734 7441 • Men can also be fitted in N.Y.C., D.C., Chicago, Boston, P.B., Dallas and S.F. • www.h-huntsman.com

How much? From £3,657/$6,600

Henry Huntsman established his business in 1849, specializing in breeches. The company was one of the first to receive a royal warrant, which was bestowed upon them in 1865 by the then Prince of Wales. Huntsman's bespoke suits manage to stay abreast of current fashion trends, while maintaining a heritage of fine craftsmanship.

*" **B** espoke v. Past tense and a past participle of bespeak. adj. 1. Custom-made. Said especially of clothes. 2. Making or selling custom-made clothes: a bespoke tailor."*

Bespoke on a budget

Traditional British brand Gieves & Hawkes (1 Savile Row, London W1; www.gievesandhawkes.com) provides a personal tailoring service which combines its ready-to-wear skills with your own requirements. At about $1,400 for a two-piece suit, it's around a quarter of the price of a bespoke suit. Irish tailor Jonathan Quearney (7 Windmill St, London W1; www.jonathanquearney.com) is also a master at whipping up a fine suit on a budget, and will make one to measure for well under $2,000. If it's classic Savile Row style you require but don't have the funds for, head to David Saxby at vintage suit emporium Old Hat (66 Fulham Rd, London SW6), who will have you kitted out in the finest second-hand suit he can lay his hands on. Another option is to simply go ready-to-wear—our favorites currently include the razor-sharp styling of Etro, Prada and Jil Sander.

ORIGINS OF SAVILE ROW

Mayfair's long association with tailoring goes back to the late 1500s, when Robert Baker set up the street's first tailoring business and named it Piccadilly after the pickadil, an Elizabethan shirt collar. Savile Row grew out of Lord Burlington's kitchen garden in 1695 and was named after his wife, Dorothy Savile, but its first tenants were military officers and physicians. It wasn't until 1733, that the first evidence of bespoke tailoring was recorded in the *Daily Post* and credited to Beau Brummel, now known as patron saint of the bespoke suit. From then on, tailors began to flourish along the street, which, due to high rent and new businesses, has diminished somewhat to around ten authentic bespoke tailors.

Bikini

Malia Mills

Where?

1031 Lexington Ave. (212.517.7485), 220 Columbus Ave. (212.874.7200) and 199 Mulberry St. N.Y.C. • www.maliamills.com

How much?

Tops and bottoms, about $200 for both.

It may be just two minuscule pieces of Lycra but, fashion-wise, nothing causes quite as much pleasure and pain as buying a bikini. And while color, print, and shape are all important, the key thing to get right is fit.

That's where New York designer Malia Mills comes in—her bikini tops work just like a bra, each one featuring contouring seams for shape and a perfect fit; three sets of hook fastenings at the back and three different size straps, ranging from thin for small tops to thicker ones on D-cup pluses. You can adjust the strap length on your bikini top for the right amount of support. Stylish tops that cover the tummy and a few one-piece suits can also be had. The bottoms also come in a range of shapes, fits, and styles, so you can ensure you find the perfect pair to suit your shape. Dispelling the myth that only certain styles suit certain shapes, Mills and her staff take each individual as she comes. In the New York stores, her expert teams use their trained eye to size you up, try a few things out and send you out of the door with the suit of your dreams. "Everyone needs to go in with the attitude that you never know what will look good," says Mills. "You have to try on a little of everything, because you never know what might be the surprise hit. The same goes for color; while you might think that a really pale girl will look best in a dark brown, she might be the perfect ice princess in a pale lilac, especially if that suits her personality."

TOMAS MAIER

Where? 1800 West Ave., Miami Beach, FL 33139 • 888.373.0707 • www.tomasmaier.com • Department stores worldwide • www.net-a-porter.com

How much? From $280

Plain but sexy shapes, bold colors, and modern techno-fabrics—Maier is particularly good for a fine bandeau bikini.

Malia Mills

ERES

Where? 2 Rue Tronchet, Paris •
621 Madison Ave. (212.223.
3550) and 98 Wooster St.
(212.431.7300), N.Y.C. •
www.eresparis.com •
Other stores in U.S and France
How much? From· $175/€143
These bikinis are subtle,
streamlined and constructed
from a unique body-contouring
stretch fabric in a range of
colors with simple shapes and
an excellent fit.

*" **Y**ou know a bikini fits
just right when you feel
great: you want the bottom to be
nice and smooth (if the fabric is
wrinkling or bunching in the
back, it's too big). You should be
able to really move around in
your top. Lift your arms up, and
make sure you don't come out of
the bottom. Bend over like
you're picking up a towel and
make sure you don't fall out. The
one thing that you want to avoid
is sacrificing fit for fashion."*

Malia Mills gives her expert advice
on how to find the perfect bikini

Eres

A SHORT BIOGRAPHY OF THE BIKINI

Ever since the two-piece swimsuit, named after an A-bomb testing site called Bikini Atoll, was pioneered by engineer Louis Reard and fashion designer Jacques Heim in Paris in the mid-1940s, it has been one of the most important garments a woman needs to get right. Brigitte Bardot propelled it into the public eye when she was snapped frolicking around in a cream sculpted bikini in 1957's *And God Created Woman*; then Ursula Andress furthered its profile a few years later as the mighty Honey Ryder in *Doctor No*. In the 1970s, Norma Kamali injected disco glamor and introduced the thong bottom, which became an instant hit on the beaches of Rio. The 1980s saw power swimwear as worn by the athletically toned Cindy Crawford, while a decade later, the pared-down simplicity of a neutral-toned Calvin Klein bikini was the ultimate in chic. But where does that leave us now? Well, with more choice, fabrics and designs than ever before. Today, we have extensive, attractive bikini ranges in a multitude of shapes from the string to the classic triangle, available everywhere, from chains such as H&M, Gap and Topshop, to high-end designers like Pucci, Missoni and Dolce & Gabbana.

Boxer shorts

Calvin Klein's Simply Smooth boxers

Where?
Department stores worldwide •
www.figleaves.com

How much?
$15-$20

Calvin Klein's Simply Smooth boxers

Compared to women, men get a raw deal when it comes to the choice of underwear on offer—it's limited, lacking in quality, and often bland as can be. Luckily, there are a few brands that have made it their mission to create simple and stylish good-quality smalls. It was 1982 when Calvin Klein first launched his now-famous boxer shorts. This prompted the trend for rap artists to reveal the waistband, making men's underwear a major fashion statement for the first time ever. Still hugely popular, the classic Calvin Klein boxer short, available simply in black, white or grey, remains the number one choice for men across the world.

ZIMMERLI ROYAL CLASSIC

Where? www.amazon.com
How much? From $65

This Swiss luxury underwear brand favored by Prince Charles, Tom Cruise and Karl Lagerfeld has been at the forefront of developing mercerized cotton (a process whereby cotton thread is covered in polyester and treated in sodium hydroxide for extra lustre and strength). Its Royal Classic boxers are the ultimate in style and comfort.

HANRO

Where? visit www.Hanro.com for a list of retailers • www.figleaves.com
How much? $50–$65

These luxurious Swiss-made mercerized cotton boxer shorts in a classic, very simple style are comfortable and cool, featuring an all-important supportive front and soft, elasticated waistband. Sleek and stylish.

And for the best swim trunks . . .

Where? Six company shops in U.S., including Southampton, N.Y., and Palm Beach, FL, and other high-end beachwear boutiques • www.vilebrequin.com
How much? From $150

While women have a thousand and one bikini brands to choose from (see pages 14–15) the choice of men's swimwear is limited and ranges from classic Speedos to tiger-print Versace—both equally awkward on the wrong physique. A much safer option is to go for classic surfer shorts. Quicksilver and Mambo are good choices for teens and twentysomethings, and Hackett offers more grown-up styles for guys. But the best quality swimming trunks can be found at Vilebrequin, which offers six different shapes, ranging from its long Okoa style to the boxer-short shaped Malibu. They come in 80 designs from renditions of Aloha prints and sea horses to classic checks.

Vilebrequin

Bra

Cadolle's Cara

Where?
255 Rue Saint Honoré, Paris • www.cadolle.com

How much?
$680/€555

One simply *must* buy one's underwear in Paris, the city of lovers and the location of the world's largest lingerie department, found in Galeries Lafayette. French women understand the importance of good underwear, that it gives you confidence, makes you feel super-sexy and ready to conquer the world. And nothing is more important than a bra that fits properly—a good one should change the appearance of your entire upper body. Alice Cadolle offers a unique made-to-measure bra service. Famous clients have included the legendary double agent Mata Hari, for whom a metal bra was created, Coco Chanel, who requested a chest-flattening design, as well as Catherine Deneuve, Brigitte Bardot and Christina Onassis. The *atelier* is located at the end of a courtyard, near the Hotel Costes, and looks like a scene straight out of the classic Audrey Hepburn movie *Funny Face*—think red velvet curtains and

Alice Cadolle shop front in Paris

assistants with tape measures strewn around their necks. The boutique is now run by Poupie—her great-great grandmother was the inventor of the bra and her mother, Alice, became famous for the made-to-measure service. Poupie has retained the company's heritage, as well as its devotion to quality, and her loyal customers come from all over the world. "The English love eccentricity while the French love tradition and good taste," she explains. "Americans are very boring—they just want nude."

The Cara, an everyday bra, is Poupie's attempt to reverse the trend for round, tennis-ball breasts, spurred on by the boom in plastic surgery. "I want to reinvent the bra and create the perfect bust," she explains. With the Cara, the breasts point from the bottom up and the back is low for support. "The back needs to be low so the front goes up. You need rigid seams and rigid straps. I only use elastic at the back… Seamless bras don't support—they're a killer. In ten years time, my clients will be the women who've been wearing seamless bras!"

At least two fittings are required over a six-week period, and Poupie can conjure up whatever a client desires. Silk is the least effective fabric for a bra, nylon netting the best, and Cadolle has 60 different shades to choose from and 50 different types of lace.

LA PERLA
Where? 38 Avenue Rd., Toronto and dozens in U.S. (17 in California) • Check www.FashionTraveler.com for locations • Plus 2 discount outlets: Orlando Premium Outlets, FL and Woodbury Common, N Y
How much? From about $50 per piece at La Perla boutiques, much less at outlets.
The Italian luxury label is best for decorating small breasts. Think sexy lace and elegant silk fabrics—particularly their Black Label range. No wonder men make up 30 per cent of all La Perla's customers.

BRAVISSIMO

Where? Stores nationwide in the U.K. • www.bravissimo.com

How much? £21/$38

Bravissimo is the best—nay, a godsend—for bigger busts. The company was founded by Sara Tremellen in 1995, when she became pregnant and couldn't find a bra to fit. They stock a wide range of cup sizes, from D to JJ, and their bras come in a variety of different shapes, styles and colors.

BRASSIERE BASICS

Rigby & Peller, corsetières to the Queen, are famous for their crack squad of fitters, who can tell the size of a woman's bra just by looking at her breasts. Indeed, their shop assistants are known to refuse to sell ill-fitting bras. Rigby & Peller, 22A Conduit St, London, W1, www.rigbyandpeller.com.

"Around 75 per cent of all women are wearing the wrong size bra. Walking down the street I see so many women whose breasts hang too low—this seems the most common problem. Whatever you may have heard, it's impossible to work out your bra size at home using a tape measure. Instead, go for a professional fitting at a reputable lingerie store and try on as many different styles as possible. The perfect bra should be snug around the ribcage. If it's too big round the back, the breasts are too low; too small round the cup, you will have four bosoms instead of two; too small around the back and it will hurt. The right bra should run in one line around your body. The underwiring should lie behind the breast tissue, almost under the armpit.

One way of checking if your bra fits is to do the finger test: place your index finger under your bra and run it round your body. If your bra starts riding up, the size is too big. Some women blame falling straps on sloping shoulders. Again, this is a sign of an ill-fitting bra. A good bra should never fall off the shoulders.

Many women's bra sizes fluctuate during the month. I recommend getting different bra sizes for different periods—if you value your breasts and don't want them to sag, this is a wise investment. Also, women should never wear wires while pregnant as their breasts are continually growing. The bra needs to be able to grow with the breast tissue—underwiring prevents this. Bras have a life of around two years and need to be handwashed. After that, throw them away!"

Jill Kenton, owner of Rigby & Peller

Giselle lingerie from Rigby & Peller

Rigby & Peller

Cashmere sweater

Loro Piana v-neck sweater

Where?

821 Madison Ave., N.Y.C., and Piana boutiques in Aspen, Coral Gables, Palm Beach, Chicago, Costa Mesa, S.F., Manhasset, Short Hills. •
www.loropiana.com

How much?

Near $700

Loro Piana is cashmere's holy grail. According to buyers and textile snobs alike, it's the very best money can buy, and the label every aficionado worth their Ralph Lauren cable-knit (another classic) aspires to. If only it weren't so darned expensive. Yet with Loro Piana, feeling really is believing—the eyebrow-rising prices are the result of Loro Piana's stringent quality control. The company only uses the purest white cashmere, the most rare and therefore the most covetable, from the Kel goat, which is found in remote high-altitude regions of Central Asia. The higher the altitude, the finer the yarn—or so the theory goes. The Italian family firm was started in the 18th century in Trivero, an Italian center for textiles, and it is now run by two very dapper brothers, Pier Luigi and Sergio Loro Piana. As well as its own-brand collection—the company's wraps and men's suits also come highly recommended—and so is its bespoke service. Loro Piana is the world's largest cashmere producer and supplies fabric for labels as diverse as Jil Sander, Giorgio Armani and J. Crew.

Loro Piana v-neck sweater

Lucien Pellat-Finet

PRINGLE V-NECK SWEATER

Where? 112 New Bond St., London W1 •
Saks Fifth Ave. • www.pringlescotland.com
How much? Prices from £300/$600
Pringle's trademark—a rampant Scottish lion—is
recognizable throughout the world, and the label
was the one that stylish stars of the 1950s, such as
Grace Kelly and Lauren Bacall, turned to for their
twin sets. Founded in 1815 by Robert Pringle, the
brand has been revamped in recent years and given
a fresher, more fashionable image.

LUCIEN PELLAT-FINET SWEATER

Where? 1 Rue de Montalembert, Paris •
14 Christopher St., N.Y.C., (212.255.8560) •
www.lucienpellat-finet.com
How much? $650–$3,500
A Lucien Pellat-Finet sweater screams Euroluxe and
is much more exciting than a standard black roll-
neck. Worth every penny for the wow factor and
top-notch craftsmanship, these sweaters sport
psychedelic colors and nutty motifs—think skulls,
medals, and marijuana leaves.

The Best Budget Cashmere

Where? UNIQLO, 546 Broadway (near Prince), N.Y.C. •
www.uniqlo.com
How much? From $70
Thanks to mass-production in China, cashmere—once
the apogee of sartorial luxury—is now affordable for
everyone. But with one regrettable downside: quality.
In recent consumer tests, garments that promised
"100 percent cashmere" actually contained camel hair
and—horror of horrors!—wool, a sneaky trick that
partly explains why discount cashmere never feels
quite as nice as the pricier stuff (and bobbles in the
blink of an eye). Still, we're smitten, and the best
we've found is from UNIQLO, the Japanese budget
chain that excels in great-fitting cashmere separates—
from classic V-necks to long-length cardies—in a
fantastic range of colors. Oprah agrees. She told
readers of her magazine, "Check out the prices of
these delicious cashmere sweaters then shop your
heart out." It's worth remembering, though, that
cheap cashmere pieces will never last as long as
garments made in Italy or Scotland. With cashmere, it
would seem, you really do get what you pay for.

*" I vividly remember the first time I paid thousands
of dollars for cashmere. It was ten years ago in
LA and I bought a lilac Lucien Pellat Finet sweater with
a huge green marijuana leaf on it from Fred Segal. It
cost me $2,800 and it was the ultimate in fuck-you
glamor. Since them I've collected them—I bought the
tiger print one, the leopard print one and the skull one.
I buy a couple a year—I must have at least 20 by now.
I love the fact they are luxurious but have a sense of
humor. I don't want to be walking around in beige or
taupe cashmere—I'll leave that to someone else!*

*What I love about cashmere is that it breathes—it
keeps you warm when it's cold but you can also wear it
to the beach so it's great for travelling. It's the ultimate
in relaxed chic—you can just sling it on over a thin
T-shirt or wear it directly against your skin. You can't
do that with lambswool."*

Patrick Cox, London-based shoe designer, on why he loves
Lucien Pellat Finet.

CASHMERE THAT LASTS A LIFETIME

To dry-clean or not to dry-clean, that is the question many a cashmere fan must ponder. Shyama Fernardo from the Cashmere Clinic (11 Beauchamp Place, London W1, 207 584 9806), the only place the well-heeled ladies of West London trust with their two-ply, offers some tips:

• "Some people are good at washing cashmere, some people are bad—it's as simple as that. You should find out what you are—if you're bad, take your garments to a cashmere professional.

• You have to be careful and cherish your cashmere, otherwise it will be ruined. We send our clients' garments to Scotland, as their cashmere heritage means they're the best people for the job.

• I would never advise anyone to dry-clean their cashmere as the chemicals will shorten its life. Instead, wash on either a cool wash or handwash cycle using Woolite—but only a little—or a mild, baby shampoo.

• Once the cashmere has been slowly spun, gently squeeze out a little before reshaping and drying it flat on a towel.

• Handwashing is not as effective, as you need to get rid of all the water, which requires patience; if soap remains, the cashmere will be matted.

• As for the perennial problem of stretching, the only way to get cashmere back to its original size is to wash it. During the process, it will shrink."

And for the perfect pashmina?

Where? Tashia, 178 Walton St., London • In U.S., at Saks Fifth Ave. and many boutiques.

"The best pashminas are woven in Katmandu, Nepal. They are much better quality than the cheap machine-woven ones from India.

The perfect fabric mixture is 65 per cent cashmere and 35 per cent silk. If the fabric is too soft the shawl will start bobbling. If it has too much silk, the shawl will be too shiny. Tassels are also very important. Too thick is downright nasty and too thin is cheap looking. The Nepalese tassles are rolled by hand, rather like cigars! Taking care of your pashmina is also important. The worst thing you can do is dry-clean or machine-wash it. To keep it looking gorgeous, handwash in warm water with shampoo then roll and lay flat."

Sara Chiaramonte of Tashia

Tashia Pashminas

Jeans for women

Earnest Cut & Sew

Where?
821 Washington St., N.Y.C. •
212.242.3414 • www.earnestsewn.com •
Holt Renfrew, 10 Canadian locations from
Ste-Foy to Vancouver • Visit
www.HoltRenfrew.com for addresses

How much?
From U.S. $280

What is it about jeans? They're so simple, yet so desirable; they are both everyday and the height of glamor, gliding from the office to cocktail bar with just a few accessory changes. In fact, denim is now so alluring that we live in an age when it's not unusual to part with $200 on a pair of jeans—make that $500+ if you want made-to-measure. But which jeans are the most coveted of them all? Remember, like perfume and bikinis, buying jeans is a highly personal thing—different brands and shapes suit different people and it's all about trying them on. However, there are some jeans out there that are guaranteed to fulfil all desires. These are the styles and brands, for men and women, that shine above the rest in terms of quality, fit and wash.

A few years ago, New York-based Scott Morrison, former co-founder/designer of Paper Denim & Cloth, set about trying to establish the finest jeans brand in the world—the result was Earnest Cut & Sew. Fusing the garment's American workwear origins with the ancient Japanese style asthetic Wabi Sabi, the range includes high-quality denim and superior cuts. And if you're not taken with the luscious cigarette-style slim jeans, you can get your very own pair made-to-measure, a service available at the New York store, Barneys, and at Selfridges, London, where you decide which cut, buttons, rivets, thread color, and back pocket you would like. The quest for the perfect jeans might just be over.

Earnest Sewn Harlan

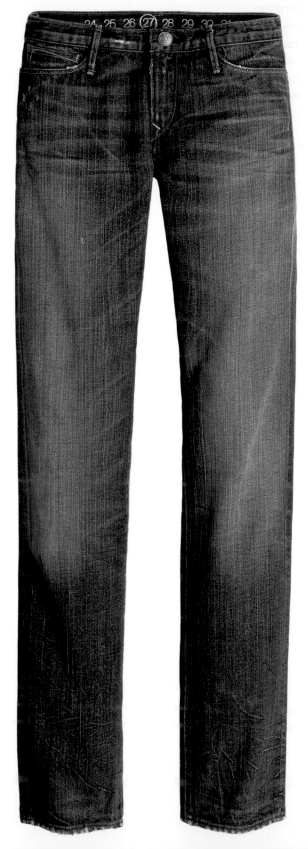

CITIZENS OF HUMANITY

Where? Bloomingdales, Nordstrom, Holt Renfrew
How much? About $200

Created by Jerome Dahan, formerly of Seven, Citizens of Humanity's jeans have a low-rise waistband, but not too low, and are accommodating around the hips, thighs and bottom, making the legs seem miraculously thinner. The Elle is a tight-fitting stretch jean in a lovely dark wash, while the Naomi is a slim-fitting bootleg that flatters most figures.

SEVEN FOR ALL MANKIND

Where? Neiman Marcus, Bloomingdales and others • Holt Renfrew in Canada.
How much? From U.S. $260

Seven For All Mankind jeans

When Seven jeans burst onto the scene in 2000, they became an instant hit, due to the remarkably slimming cut. Now, despite numerous new competitors, Seven jeans, with "For All Mankind" added to the moniker, remain ultra-desirable thanks to the simple, flattering silhouette, and deep-blue washes.

Both Citizens and Seven jeans are sometimes found on www.bluefly.com, for as much as 40 per cent off.

" I wish I had invented blue jeans... Jeans are expressive and discreet, they have sex appeal and simplicity—everything I could want for the clothes I design. "

Yves Saint Laurent

" Jeans are your most important piece of clothing, no question. They have to be worn. And they've got to be old. I also prefer that they be button-fly. The right jeans and a T-shirt can be sexier than the most expensive tailored suit. "

Donna Karan

The best...

Skinny jeans are by Acne, Notify, and Superfine; they're good on lean and gamine types. At Barneys, Bergdorf's (N.Y.C.) and www.vibetheboutique.com

White jeans are by James Cured by Sewn—the five pocket stretch cord rocks. Surprisingly flattering. Available at www.shopbop.com, www.shopLAstyle.com

Cropped jeans are by Citizens of Humanity—the cropped "Kelly" stretch is the one you're after. See above.

All-round flattering jeans are Paige Denim's Laurel Canyon five-pocket stretch, thanks to lean styling, a permanent crease at the front, and well-placed pockets. Available at Neiman Marcus, www.soliscompany.com

Sassy LA jeans are by Serfontaine, Blue Cult and Juicy Couture; excellent for curvy girls. Neiman Marcus for LA Jeans, www.shopzilla.com or www.bluefly.com for others.

Rock and roll cool jeans are by True Religion due to their slouchy fit, funky pocket stitching, and distressed detailing. Neiman Marcus, www.ADASA.com

Deconstructed jeans with a modern edge are by Ødyn, a relatively new Swedish brand that offers a fresh look and nice antidote to all those LA brands. Available at www.revolveclothing.com.

Jeans for men

Rogan

Where?
www.rogannyc.com • Fred Segal, 8100 Melrose
Ave., Los Angeles • 500 Broadway, Santa Monica
How much?
From $335

Rogan jeans

Rogan Gregory set up his company a few years back, with the aim of creating a denim range using top-quality yarns and washes with a social and environmental purpose. His wonderfully well-designed Original jeans are one of the sexiest, coolest, and best-fitting styles men can buy, made with fine dyes, excellent tailoring and limited editions designed by Max Fenton.

PAPER DENIM & CLOTH

Where? Fred Segal stores (see above) , Louis of Boston, Scoop boutiques and good department stores. •
www.paperdenim.com
How much? From $300
This brand, favored by Tom Cruise, features jeans that are just the right fit—slim, but with a hint of bagginess, and good on the backside (i.e. not too low)—which makes them among the most wearable jeans out there. The recently launched BMX fit, a five-pocket model with a full, straight leg, is particularly appealing.

EVISU

Where? Lounge, 155 John St. and Sweet 99, 99 Spadine Ave., Toronto. • Visit website for a list of U.S. boutiques: www.evisu.com
How much? From $250
This top-quality Japanese brand, born in a tiny tailor shop in Osaka, Japan, now delivers some of the best-quality denims in the world. The iconic Japanese label is designed by Burberry alumnus, Johnny Diamandis, and now features a new rainbow logo to prevent counterfeits.

THE DEVIL IS IN THE DETAILS

You can tell a lot about the quality of a pair of jeans by looking at the details. The **selvage** is the white stripe running down the seam, which seals the edge of the denim to prevent it fraying—experts can tell the brand and quality of the denim just by looking at this; New Yorkers actually show them off by rolling their jeans up. **Rivets** are the little metal studs used to reinforce the pockets and prevent wear and fraying. The **rise** is the distance between the crotch and the waistband. In many ways, the **back pocket** is now more important than the cut—it's the telltale sign of the brand and the position is instrumental in flattering the bottom. **Washes** are getting ever more complex, the older and more worn your jeans look, whether through sandblasting, rock washing or punching with holes, the more expensive they are likely to be.

CULT CLASSIC: LEVI'S 501S

Who hasn't owned a pair of trusty old Levi's 501s at some point? They are, without doubt, the most classic and iconic jeans ever and while not exactly the height of fashion, the Levi's 501 will probably be around for much longer than many of the flashy young jeans currently on the market. Levi Strauss was a Jewish Bavarian immigrant who hooked up with tailor Jacob Davis in San Francisco to create men's trousers that wouldn't rip. Jacob had the brainwave of introducing rivets at points of strain, like on the pocket corners and base of the button fly. Although denim originates from 17th century France, and American men had worn denim trousers without rivets for much of the 19th century, 1873—the year Levi Strauss & Co. patented denim jeans with rivets—is viewed as the official birth date of blue jeans. The number 501 was assigned to the jeans in 1890 and the red tab was added in 1936 to help identify them from a distance. The double row stitching on the back pockets, known as the Arcuate stitching design, is the oldest apparel trademark still in use today; it was first used in 1873 and during the Second World War, when it was painted on the pockets due to government rationing of essential items such as thread. Since 1966, reinforced stitching has replaced the back pocket rivets. A Levi's red tab with a capital E indicates they are pre-1971. Levi's bought a pair of 1890 501s for $25,000 in 1997. Today, a typical pair of 501s takes 3¼ yards of denim, five buttons, six rivets, and 37 separate sewing operations.

Still stuck for choice?

Bodymetrics Have your body scanned using "virtual fashion" technology to determine the perfect-fitting jeans. Selfridges, 400 Oxford St., London W1, and branches • 020 8708 377 377

Barneys "Jeans Genies" will help you find the jeans of your dreams. www.barneys.com

Cantaloup Destination Denim on New York's Upper East Side carries innovative labels like Tsubi, Sacred Blue, and Oligo Tissew. 1359 Second Ave., N.Y.C.• 212.288.3569

Fred Segal is a jeans haven in L.A., the epicenter for jeans production. The original store is at 8100 Melrose Ave., Los Angeles • 323.655.3784

Henri Bendel's "Denim Dream Team" will get you kitted out with divine denim. 712 Fifth Ave. at 56th St., N.Y.C. • 212.247.1100

Brix Smith-Start at Shoreditch boutique Start can usually find you the jeans of your dreams just by looking at you. 59 Rivington St., London EC2

Panties

Agent Provocateur

Where?

7961 Melrose Ave., L.A., 133 Mercer St., N.Y.C., Caesar's Forum shops, Las Vegas • www.agentprovocateur.com

How much?

From $45

For women, a pair of knickers is one of the most personal, secretive, and exciting of purchases. Agent Provocateur, who made spending upwards of $30 on a pair of panties acceptable, still offers one of the most pleasurable knicker-buying experiences thanks to their well-trained staff and exquisitely sexy selection. Established by Vivienne Westwood's son Joe Corre and his girlfriend Serena Rees in 1994, with the aim of creating the perfect lingerie store, Agent Provocateur's first shop in London's Broadwick Street is glamorous and stylish. The finely made silk and lace knickers are still some of the best you can find.

Agent Provocateur

SABBIA ROSA

Where? 71–73 Rue des Saints-Pères, 75006, Paris

How much? From $60/€50

This elegant French lingerie shop has served the likes of Madonna, Kate Moss and Catherine Deneuve, who no doubt adore the fine silk smalls and exquisite handmade lingerie. Naomi Campbell often buys up the whole collection. This label is luxurious to the max and super indulgent.

LA PERLA

Where? La Perla boutiques are throughout the U.S. and in Toronto (see page 17).

How much? From about $50

This Italian brand makes panties in top-quality lace and pleated tulle, with a cinematic glamor and screen-star appeal in sexy black or more neutral beiges and creams.

The world's most comfortable pants

If it's simply a fabulously flattering pair of panties you're after, the kind that won't expose any lumps and bumps or peep above the waistband of jeans and skirts, we have three recommendations. **Cosabella** (www.cosabella.com) is an Italian brand that produces the archetypal knicker shape in sheer colors, while **Elle Macpherson Intimates** (www.ellemacphersonintimates.com) do a fantastic low-slung range that flatters the figure to no end. British company **Bodas** (www.bodas.co.uk) also offers an excellent range of neutrally toned knickers with minimal seams to prevent the dreaded VPL.

Little black dress

Lanvin

Where?
22 Rue du Fauborg St-Honoré, Paris • www.lanvin.com
How much?
From $1,500

Jeanne Lanvin set up as a milliner in Paris in 1889 and went on to become one of the leading female couturiers of the early 19th century, her name synonymous with a pure, feminine style of chic. Lanvin excelled at designing beautiful dresses for mothers and daughters and was known for the "robe de style:" a dress with a dropped waist and full skirt. Fast-forward to the next century and Israeli designer Albert Elbaz has revived the label's appeal—albeit with a dash of urban modernity—in his role as artistic director. This award-winning designer studied at the Tel Aviv School of Fashion and Textiles, trained in New York under the watchful eye of society-couturier, Geoffrey Beene, and made his name as artistic director at Yves Saint Laurent in 1998. He has proved that, just like Jeanne Lanvin, he has an instinct for creating divine dresses and, most importantly, the ultimate little black dress (LBD). His flattering, cinch-waist LBDs, a favourite with the red carpet contingent, appear effortless, and fit the female form to perfection.

CHANEL
Where? Chanel fashion stores • www.chanel.com • in U.S. & Canada, Bloomingdales, Neiman Marcus, Hershleifer, Holt Renfrew
How much? From $1,500
Karl Lagerfeld keeps the spirit of Coco Chanel and the LBD heritage alive (see box overleaf) by designing around six new styles each season from simple shifts to body-skimming gowns. A Chanel LBD is an investment for life.

DIANE VON FURSTENBERG
Where? DVF stores in N.Y.C, L.A., & Miami • department stores in U.S. & Canada • www.bluefly.com
How much? From $245
"Feel like a woman, wear a dress!" exclaimed Diane von Furstenberg in the early 1970s as she shot to fashion super-stardom after creating the now iconic jersey wrap dress. Thirty years on and the Belgian designer is still creating classic dresses—including about eight brilliant variations on the LBD each season from slinky wrap-around styles to neat shifts.

> **"A** *dress can be the expression of a state of mind. There are dresses that sing of joy of life, dresses that weep, dresses that threaten. There are gay dresses, mysterious dresses, pleasing dresses, and tearful dresses."*
>
> **Paul Poiret, designer, 1879–1944**

Lanvin's belted LBD

Chanel LBD

Diane von Furstenberg's LBD

THE ORIGINS OF THE LITTLE BLACK DRESS

In 1919, Coco Chanel put black in fashion. Seven years later, *American Vogue* illustrated the Chanel "Ford," calling it the "frock that all the world would wear." It was a sleeveless, black crepe-de-chine dress with a pin-tucked front, and thus the little black dress was born. Many have evolved the look. In the 1950s, French couturier, Jacques Fath, created elegant dresses to flatter the hourglass figure; in the 1960s, the LBD became truly fashionable once more with the space-age mini-dress look, epitomized by Twiggy and designer Paco Rabanne. In the late 1960s and 1970s, British designer Jean Muir made the "little nothing" of a black dress a classic. As she said: "When you have found something that suits you and never lets you down, why not stick to it?"

Nowadays, it's not only Karl Lagerfeld, Albert Elbaz and Diane von Furstenberg pushing the LBD into the 21st century with style and grace, but a new generation of savvy dress designers including Georgina Chapman and Kerin Craig for the A-lister's favourite Marchesa (available at www.neimanmarcus.com), and Narciso Rodriquez (available at www.net-a-porter.com). Long may it live.

www.thatperfectlittleblackdress.com
A brilliant website that sells a well-edited selection of elegant vintage black dresses from the 1940s to 1990s.

Pajamas

Derek Rose

Where?
15 Savile Row, London W1 •
www.derek-rose.com
How much?
From £99.99/$180

Derek Rose

We're currently in the grip of a pajama boom. Thanks to the recent trend for "relaxation" gear and men rediscovering the joys of nightwear, sales rose by over 20 per cent in 2004. Derek Rose is the undisputed king of pjs. His collection is worn by everyone from the Queen to the children at Hogwarts in the *Harry Potter* films—even John and Yoko had matching his-and-hers pairs.

The Savile Row company, which was founded in 1926, specializes in tailored pajamas—a flattering and generous cut, an elastic waist, and a draught-proof array of buttons—in essence everything you could want from the perfect pajama. The blue satin stripe with a single pocket and white piping is its bestseller, and since the company started a woman's line, the pink satin stripe is doing a roaring trade, too. The key is Rose's insistence that the satin is made from two-fold yarn, which gives the cloth more depth as well as ensuring it lasts longer. Also popular are the company's silk designs—*very* Cary Grant—as well as the military-influenced Regimental Stripe collection: with names like Black Watch and Brigade of Guards. After all, at some point everyone ends up a weekend guest—and 4 a.m. visits to the bathroom in a faded Snoopy T-shirt just won't do.

LAURENCE TAVERNIER
Where? 32 Rue du Bac, Paris • Saks Fifth Ave, N.Y.C. and other cities •
www.laurencetavernier.com
How much? From $180/€159
This French luxury label is dedicated to nightwear, making soft, cotton pajamas, which are surprisingly elegant, yet still comfortable; as well as woollen bed coats, cashmere robes, slippers, and bed socks. A range that is chic enough to wear outside the house—just about.

BROOKS BROTHERS
Where? 346 Madison Ave. • 212.682.8800 • branches in Manhattan, throughout the U.S. and world, and U.S. discount outlets • www.brooksbrothers.com
How much? $70
Brooks Brothers' candy-stripe pajamas are the ones Madonna wore when photographed at home in bed with her children—in matching pairs—for *Vogue*. Perfectly preppy, they're made from soft cotton with a darker blue piping and a drawstring waist.

Raincoat

Burberry trenchcoat

Where?
21-23 New Bond St., London • branches in 13 U.S. states, and Holt Renfrew
How much?
From £695/$1,280

It's hard to pinpoint exactly what makes the Burberry raincoat such a timeless classic—the hint of checked lining perhaps? The simple belted form? The smart military epaulettes? In the early 1900s, British army officers started wearing these coats as part of their uniform, and, by the 1940s, the trenchcoat had filtered into mainstream fashion. Today, the Burberry coat is still made from a closely woven Egyptian cotton called gabardine. It remains the best-loved raincoat there is, with all its authentic details still intact, such as the metal D-rings on the belt. Burberry's current Creative Director, Christopher Bailey, updates the style each season, reviving it with long or short hemlines, in a variety of colors and fabrics, including luxurious leather, suede, and tweed. And, for the ultimate raincoat, you can now get your very own bespoke Burberry trench, made up to your specific shape and size. You can even get your intials embroidered onto the lining.

Burberry trenchcoat

MACINTOSH
Where? 54–55 Burlington Arcade, London W1
How much? From £495/$885
Created in the late 19th century, Macintosh is the original waterproof coat, made from a waterproof woollen fabric that was patented in 1829 by Charles Macintosh and Charles Goodyear. The classic British company now offers a made-to-measure service at the flagship London store.

AQUASCUTUM
Where? 100 Regent St., London • 450 Boylston St., Boston • 1307 Ste. Catherine St. W., Montreal
How much? About £650 or U.S. $1,600
In 1851, John Emary opened a small, high-quality tailors shop on Regent Street and in 1883 created the first rain-repellent cloth, naming it Aquascutum, taken from the Latin for water and shield, which subsequently became the name of his clothing brand. Emary went on to make a coat for King Edward VII in the late 1890s and then created trenchcoats for soldiers—and Winston Churchill. The contemporary Aquascutum range includes modern takes on the classic trench, but if it's a traditional style you're after, go for the classic Kingsgate design, available in navy, dark beige, and black.

Shirt

Charvet

Where?
28 Place Vendôme, Paris •
Holt Renfrew in several Canadian
cities

How much?
Bespoke shirts from
approximately U.S.$200

Housed in an elegant seven-floor building in Paris' Place Vendôme, Charvet is undisputedly the center of the universe for shirt aficionados. Apart from the fact that it is reputed to have the largest selection of shirt fabrics in the world—they have 400 different shades of white and at least 200 different blues to choose from—the cut is impeccable. With its squared-off bottom, smart collar, elegant cuffs, and solid buttons, a Charvet shirt looks as good with a bespoke suit as it does under a lambswool v-neck sweater.

Charvet's fine cotton shirts

TURNBULL & ASSER

Where? 71 & 72 Jermyn St., London • 42 E. 57 St., N.Y.C • 9633 Beverly Hills, CA • www.turnbullandasser.com

How much? From £140/$255: minimum of six shirts for first order.

Worn by prime ministers and princes alike (it's rumored that the Sultan of Oman ordered 240 shirts in 20 minutes), this renowned British label was established in 1885. Choose from 1,000 different cloths, ranging from plain white poplin to voile, and brushed cotton to silk. What sets these shirts apart from the competition is the classic deep-spread collar, three-button barrel cuff, white lining, and deep buffalo-horn buttons.

SIMONE ABBARCHI

Where? Borgo Santissimi Apostoli 16, Borgo Santissimi, Florence, Italy

How much? From $100/€122

The Italian tailor makes 3,000 shirts a year and has a loyal client base from London to L.A. Customers start with a 25-minute consultation, during which measurements are taken and sample swatches shown. All the shirts are made exclusively from Italian cotton, linen and silk.

Silk

Jim Thompson Thai Silk Company

Where?

9 Surawong Rd., Bangkok • 1694 Chantilly Dr., Atlanta • Asia Society Gift Shop, 725 Park Ave., N.Y.C. • Teilo & Cie, 1407 Rue de la Montague, Montreal • www.jimthompson.com

How much?

From $150 per meter

There's a wealth of choice at the Xiushui Silk Market in Beijing or at Varanasi in India, where many of the silks are interwoven with golden thread, but if you're serious about silk shopping, nowhere beats Thailand. Thai silk may be rougher in texture and heavier than silk made in China or India, but its quality is second to none, thanks to the country having the best soil in which to cultivate mulberry bushes (the leaves of which make up a silkworm's diet) and because the producers maximize the length of time a cocoon is boiled.

American Jim Thompson's name and shop are part of Thai legend, the rolls of silk displayed according to shade and hue and sold by the yard. For anyone after the finished product, there are also cushions, bedspreads, silk box-lamps that glow like candles and a selection of ready-to-wear dresses, shirts, and ties. For something more bespoke, buy Thompson silk here and then take it to one of the hundreds of tailors dotted around Bangkok.

Jim Thompson's Thai shop has recently undergone a facelift, its slick new interior the work of hot, London-based designer Ou Baholyodhin. Ou is also behind a range of butter-soft leather goods in sugared-almond shades, as well as silk cushions, quilts, and wooden furniture. Ou's items are often used in shoots for international design magazines.

And if that wasn't enough, the top floor is devoted to Thai antiques, everything from intricately carved miniature boxes to chests of drawers fit for a palace bedroom. Jim Thompson has also branched out into stylish bars, opening a number around Bangkok, thus further spreading the word in tasteful Thai living. For the ardent bargain hunter, there's a Jim Thompson factory outlet at Sukhumvit Soi 93.

Jim Thompson's Kaleidoscope

Jim Thompson's Sathorn

Jim Thompson's Paradise

Jim Thompson's Venus new silk twill

OCKPOPTOK

Where? www.ockpoptok.com

How much? From $9

Meaning "East meets West," this label was set up in 2000 by Jo Smith, a fashion photographer from London, and local girl, Veo Duangdala. Based in Luang Prabang, the weaving capital of Laos—where the silk is said to be of particularly high quality, all the better to take strong colors—the company uses only the finest silks and best quality natural dyes. OckPopTok has local weavers make up their products, which include clothes, wall hangings, and cushions. No wonder their client list boasts Mick Jagger.

SHANGHAI TANG

Where? Ala Moana Shopping Center, Honolulu • Mandarin Oriental, Miami • 600 Madison Ave., N.Y.C. • www.shanghaitang.com

How much? From $80

China's first luxury label—started by Hong Kong businessman David Tang—excels in Chinese silk. Think dresses using traditional patterns in thoroughly modern colors (shocking pinks and eye-popping limes).

Tie

Hermès

Where?
Hermès stores worldwide • www.hermes.com
How much?
From $175/€120

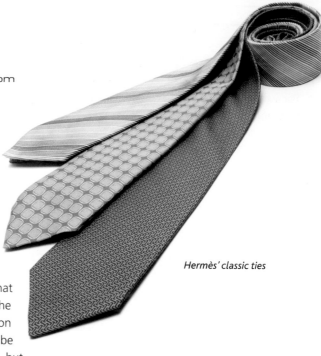

Hermès' classic ties

The tie: a curious invention and not entirely necessary. Well, it doesn't exactly serve much practical purpose now does it? The thing is, a shirt can look somewhat dull and vacant without one. A shirt and tie form an important sartorial partnership, and matching a shirt color and pattern to the tie is essential. So too is the way a collar sits on the neck (it should be neither too low nor too high), the way the knot fills the spread (so that it isn't too fat or too skinny) and the way in which the blade covers the placket of the shirt front to finish on the waistband. Then there's the texture: a tie should be good to the touch—neither too floppy nor too rigid, but in a weighty, quality silk.

The classic Hermès tie is, for men, what its silk scarves are for women: refined, traditional, and superior in quality. That discreet green and orange "Hermès" label on the back is loaded with meaning—suggesting refinement and wealth. The designs are classic with a twist and guaranteed to carry weight in the boardroom.

DUCHAMP

Where? 75 Ledbury Rd., Notting Hill, London • Barneys, N.Y.C. • Holt and Renfrew, Canada • www.duchamp.co.uk
How much? £65/$115
A relative newcomer to the tie scene, this dynamic British brand has injected a little life and soul into the market with vibrant, colorful designs made in silks of the highest quality. Duchamp has attracted quite a cult following as a result.

EMILIO PUCCI

Where? Boutiques and department stores worldwide including Neiman Marcus • www.pucci.com
How much? From $175/€118
Vibrant Italian brand, Emilio Pucci, still designs some of the most iconic of ties in its signature swirly prints. Bold, bright, and a flamboyant style statement in their own right. Search on eBay for classic and collectible 1960s' styles.

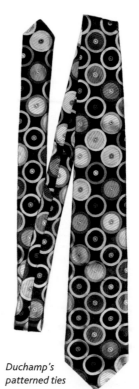

Duchamp's patterned ties

T-shirt

The plain and simple white T-shirt is probably the most widely worn garment in the world. So you would have thought it would be a cinch to find a good one, one that works in a variety of contexts and fits in all the right places—but it's not.

For women this means covering the midriff and skimming the top of your jeans with a fit that shows you have breasts without turning you into a contestant from a wet T-shirt competition. Sleeves are vital too—you don't want them to be too square and long, or you'll look like a throwback from a dodgy 1980s' pop band, and you don't want a capped sleeve, as that's not a T-shirt at all.

For guys, a T-shirt should neither be too baggy nor too tight. Ideally, you want it to hint at those sculpted pecks and leave the rest to the imagination.

T-shirts in every colour at American Apparel

T-shirt for men

Zimmerli of Switzerland

Where?

www.zimmerlitextil.ch

How much?

From $88/€71

Established in 1871 by a needlework teacher named Pauline Zimmerli-Bauerlin, this Swiss luxury underwear brand—currently worn by Prince Charles, Tom Cruise, and Karl Lagerfeld—has been at the forefront of developing the most luxurious T-shirts a man can buy. It's all down to their handling of fibres—using machines designed and made exclusively for the brand with delicate rod-twisted yarns that have been mercerized twice (a process in which the cotton thread is covered in polyester and treated in sodium hydroxide for added lustre and strength). The ultimate white T-shirt is from its "Richelieu" collection—a shirt in 100 per cent mercerized cotton. Beautifully cut, soft but strong on the skin, it is sumptuous and practical too.

Mercerized cotton T-shirt, Zimmerli of Switzerland

AMERICAN APPAREL

Where? Stores worldwide including the U.S., U.K., France, Canada, Mexico and Japan • www.americanapparel.net
How much? From $18

This cool T-shirt label's 2001 version of the fine, jersey short-sleeved classic T-shirt is slightly fitted and of a soft texture. Best of all, the label is anti-sweatshops. The ethical consumer's choice.

HANES

Where? Department stores worldwide • 1.800.254.1545 • www.hanes.com
How much? From $6

As worn by Marlon Brando, this classic American T-shirt brand's short-sleeved "Beefy T" in white features 100 per cent ringspun cotton, high-stitch density fabric and double-needled seams.

T-shirt for women

Where?
Selected department stores worldwide, including Barneys, Bergdorf Goodman, and Saks Fifth Ave. • www.candccalifornia.com
How much?
From $45

C&C California's "Classic Tee"

C&C California was founded by Los Angeles design duo Cheyann Benedict and Claire Stansfield in 2003. Their mission statement was to create the best T-shirt ever—and they've succeeded in 50 flying colors. Each of the 20 styles is made from ultra-fine combed cotton, so it moves and stretches in all the right ways, while feeling ultra-soft on the skin.

C&C's most perfect T-shirt is the "Classic Tee," which features a flattering, wider-than-usual crewneck, and also provides the perfect coverage over low-slung jeans. Lightweight and luxurious against the skin, it can be worn alone or layered beneath another. A wardrobe staple.

PETIT BATEAU

Where? 1100 Madison Ave., N.Y.C • Eurochild, La Jolla, CA, 1.877.387.6244, www.eurochild.com • Department stores, including Saks
How much? From $16

A classic French kidswear label, set up in 1893, Petit Bateau's short-sleeved, scalloped crewneck T-shirt is as plain and simple as can be, with a classic cut and quality, thickish cotton.

GAP

Where? Stores everywhere • www.gap.com
How much? From $8

Gap's "Favorite T-shirt" originated when the brand began in 1969 and remains a bestseller due to its classic cut, ample-width crewneck, just-right sleeves and durable thick white cotton.

Wedding dress

Vera Wang

Where?

Vera Wang Bridal House, 991 Madison Ave., N.Y.C. • Coastal Couture, Orange Beach, AL • Mario's, Portland, OR • Mel & Me, Cranston, RI • Jamie's, Nashville, TN • Tooties, Houston, TX • Stanley Korshal, Dallas, TX • www.verawang.com

How much?

From $2,000

Vera Wang

Since the early 1990s, Vera Wang has been the bridal label with the maximum kudos. Her dresses have a signature look, with clean lines and minimal fuss, yet they possess head-turning glamor. Wang treats the wedding aisle with the same attitude other designers treat the red carpet, and she has fittingly been the designer-of-choice for many an A-list bride—think Uma Thurman, Jessica Simpson and Sharon Stone.

Frustrated at being unable to find a suitable dress for her own wedding, Wang spotted a niche in the market. In 1990, she opened her first boutique in the glitzy uptown Carlyle Hotel in New York. The collection was an instant hit, with brides-to-be swooning over the expensive fabrics and exquisite detailing like delicate hand-sewn beading. More than anything, though, they lap up Wang's vision of the modern bride: a career woman, quite possibly older than brides of yore, looking for a suitably sophisticated and grown-up dress.

Vera Wang still has a showroom at the Carlyle, a space that's considered by many as the ultimate bridal salon. Since she now has so many imitators, all of her gowns come with a certificate of authenticity. Her Manhattan sample sales remain the stuff of legend—bridezillas have been known to travel across continents to fight tooth and claw for a heavily discounted gown, many of them one-of-a-kind.

STEWART PARVIN

Where? 14 Motcomb St., London SW1 • Bridal Accents, Savage, MN • Exclusives for the Bride, Chicago • Pure English Bridal, Virginia Beach • New England Bridal, Milford, CT • Mon Amie Bridal, Costa Mesa • www.stewartparvin.com

How much? From $3,500 for ready-made, $15,000 for bespoke

As one of the Queen's favorite designers, Parvin's well-heeled clientele know they're getting quality. His designs are strong and structured with razor-sharp lines.

Monique Lhuillier

MONIQUE LHUILLIER

Where? Bergdorf, Beverly
Hills • Edina, MN •
better bridal shops •
www.moniquelhuillier.com
How much? Approximately
$7,000
Since starting her company in
1996, Monique Lhuillier's
range of gowns—romantic,
dreamy, with a subtle
sexuality—has gone from
strength to strength. Many
have a long silk sash, adding a
welcome splash of color to the
bridal outfit.

SARTORIAL TIPS FOR THE MERINGUE-A-PHOBIC BRIDE

Browns Bride is a bridal boutique with a difference. An outpost of a famous London shop—which is itself internationally renowned for spotting up-and-coming designers—the philosophy behind Bride is no different. As well as elegant designs from Emanuel Ungaro, Badgley Mischka and Monique Lhuillier, the store stocks more fashion-forward designs: from peach, ruffled Marc Jacobs numbers (hardly the traditional bridal getup but endlessly pretty nonetheless) to the more avant-garde Comme des Garçons. In Browns Bride, (almost) anything goes. Here the boutique's owner, Caroline Burstein Collis, gives invaluable tips for the thoroughly modern bride...

• Civil weddings in City Hall or before a small-town Justice of the Peace are a great chance to break the style rules. A stunning example could be a sexy cream Alexander McQueen fitted suit, worn with a pair of Louboutin patent platform shoes in a shade of "skin."

• It's probably best not to look overly sexy on your wedding day, but if you are a sensual woman, you will want to show off this strong side of your personality— and your fiancée will love you all the more for it. For those with a fabulous figure, an Azzadine Alaia piece will show off your curves and pull you in in all the right places.

• Red is a wonderful alternative to the white wedding dress. Monique Lhuillier recently made a blood-red ball gown for one of our brides who married in Scotland at her fiancé's castle on New Year's Eve. They had snow and a sleigh to carry them away.

• Black is the other color that a few "alternative" brides go for. It is not for the faint-hearted, but I have seen it looking wonderful.

• Non-traditional names to look out for include Alberta Ferretti and Carlos Miele, who both create wedding dresses that are sensual and romantic. They are not traditional in any sense; instead, are soft and flowing with that "wow" factor, and are perfect for destination weddings since they pack easily into a small suitcase.

• Last but not least, Browns' latest wedding dress innovation is the "Emergency" wedding gown. It packs up into a roll, is made from silk jersey with a separate tulle underskirt, is crush-proof and comes with a bottle of black or red Dylon so you can dye it after the wedding and wear it again. Really, what could be more modern than that!

Food & drink

"*Eating is not merely a material pleasure. Eating well gives a spectacular joy to life and contributes immensely to goodwill and happy companionship. It is of great importance to the morale.*"

Elsa Schiaparelli, fashion designer, 1890–1973

Balsamic vinegar

Giuseppe Giusti Aceto Balsamico Tradizionale

Where?

Viale Trento Trieste, 25–41100 Modena, Italy • www.giusti1605.com •
Better food markets and gourmet websites, including Dean and Deluca
shops in New York, www.deandeluca.com, and www.clubsauce.com

How much?

From $15 for a basic vinegar to upwards of $175

*Giuseppe
Giusti*

It might seem surprising today, but balsamic vinegar wasn't on sale
commercially until the 1960s. Before then, this "black gold" was a
well-kept secret, the sole preserve of Italian housewives lucky enough to
know a decent producer. Nowadays, it's available in supermarkets all over
the world, although for the most part it isn't actually balsamic vinegar, instead, it's a
mixture of wine vinegar, caramel, and colorings, a concoction that
tastes astringent when compared to the real thing. Grapes should be the
only ingredient.

The good stuff should be as dark as treacle and almost as thick, the taste a balance of
sweet and sour. The general rule is the older the vinegar, the better. There are two key terms to look out for:
"tradizionale," which means it has been aged for at least 12 years, and "D.O.C.," meaning it comes from a controlled
denomination. You also need to check the provenance, as proper balsamic vinegar can only come from Modena in
Italy, where they have stringent rules, similar to the appellation system for wines in France. Wax stamps placed over
the corks are color-coded in relation to age: red and white for vinegars at least 12 years old, silver for at least 18 years
old, and gold for 25 years old or more. Particulary old and therefore high quality vinegars will have a distinctive short
and stocky bottle and stand.

You really can't go wrong with any aged balsamic vinegar from Modena. One of the oldest is Giusti, a family
business that has been going since the early 17th century. The whole range is recommended, in particular their 40-
year-old vintage, the perfect gift for any gourmand. Giusti's vinegar has been described as "sweet, warm, and
wooded with a tart finish." Buy from the family's Modena store, once frequented by Verdi.

LEONARDI ACETAIA BALSAMICO
Where? Good international food stores • www.manicaretti.com
How much? From approximately $30
Produced by Giovanni Leonardi, a family business established in 1871, and another good name to look for.

CAVALLI "CONDIMENTI BALSAMIC"
Where? Acetaia Ferdinando Cavalli, 6/ab Via del Cristo, Fellegaro di Scandiano, Italy • www.vendaravioli.com •
www.cooksshophere.com • Good international food stores
How much? About $17.50
Not strictly balsamic vinegar, but the best commercial balsamic "dressing" you will find. Made in Scandiano,
Cavalli uses old barrels for flavor, some dating back to the 18th century. Chefs use it for marinating and
seasoning salads.

Caviar

Almas Caviar

Where?

Various sources including: The Caviar House, 161 Piccadilly, London W1 • www.caviarhouse.com

How much?

Approximately £350/$700 for 100g (3½ oz)

The most prized caviar is also the most rare. Iranian Almas, which is pale—almost white—in color, comes from very rare albino sturgeons. Almas tastes creamy, smooth, and almost buttery, and has an 18-month waiting list at The Caviar House in Piccadilly, where it is sold in a gold tin. In Iran, in fact, this caviar used to be the preserve of the Shah—and anyone else found eating it would have their right hand chopped off.

Almas caviar

Some fine Iranian caviar can be found in the U.S. since it relaxed its trade embargo just enough to allow the importation of sturgeon roe (and rugs)—necessities of the luxe life. The *Browne Trading Company* in Portland, Maine, is a leading importer of top caviars (but alas, not Almas) and a supplier to Daniel Boulud and other world-class chefs. It's possible to buy caviar at Browne Trading's retail shop on Merrill's Wharf. Or one can browse its goods online (www.browne-trading.com) and order by telephone: 800 944 7848. Browne will ship anywhere in the U.S., but not to Canada.

Browne's top caviar is nutty and mellow, small-grained Astara Persicus produced by sturgeon whose home water is the south Caspian Sea. Imperial's U.S. market price can vary: on the day we checked, 20g could be had for $190; a kilo could be purchased for $7,200. Caviar from the Russian side of the Caspian was also available at $192 per ounce or $6,800 for a kilo.

One may also sup on caviar chez *Petrossian* in either New York, 911 Seventh Ave. (212 245 2217) or Los Angeles, 321 N. Robertson Blvd (310 271 0756). Its Iranian choice is Imperial Special Reserve Persicus; Russian and domestic choices are also possible, as is purchase at www.petrossian.com with shipment by Fedex.

The delicate nature of *any* form of caviar means it should never be touched with any metal other than gold. Instead, serve the eggs using a mother-of-pearl spoon, the traditional utensil, although a wooden or plastic one will do; 14–28g (½–1oz) per person should suffice. Great caviar is best with few if any accompaniments; other caviars may be served on blinis with sour cream. Gourmands suggest separating the caviar and sour cream, and eating each alternately on separate blinis to provide a delightful contrast. Wash down with a glass of champagne or a shot of vodka.

TSAR NICOULAI, CALIFORNIAN ESTATE OSETRA

Where? Tsar Nicoulai Caviar Cafe, 1 Ferry Building (#12), San Francisco • 415.288.8630 • www.tsarnicoulai.com
How much? About $50 for a 28g (1oz) jar
When sturgeon were discovered in Californian rivers, the U.S. caviar industry revved into action. This is an excellent choice for Americans. Osetra have larger eggs than beluga and are brown with a distinctive nutty taste.

COULD CAVIAR BE THE SECRET TO A FLAWLESS COMPLEXION?

Caviar is one of the most nutritionally complete foods—it contains 47 vitamins and minerals—and is therefore extremely good for you, especially for your skin. Skincare guru Eve Lom (she of muslin cloth fame) has been eating caviar since she was a child. "What interests me as a skincare specialist is to see the effect of caviar on my skin and hair," she says. "The oils lubricate my skin and make my hair much glossier. My interest in skin is all about texture, and no cream or cosmetic in the world is as effective as eating 50g (1½oz) of caviar. It doesn't matter if your skin is naturally dry or oily—the results are truly amazing."

Prestige selection caviar from Caviar House

Champagne

Louis Roederer Brut Premier

Louis Roederer Brut Premier

Where?

www.woodswholesalewine.com (MI) • www.wineanthology.com (NJ) • www.winerz.com (CA) • good wine stores

How much?

Approximately $35–$50

It would seem that we're all adhering to the famous creed of Lily Bollinger, who hailed from the champagne house of the same name and once said: "I drink champagne when I'm happy, and I drink it when I'm sad… otherwise I never touch it—unless I'm thirsty." Champagne consumption is higher now than ever before, especially among women, who are 13 times more likely to crack open the bubbly than men, making it no longer the preserve of special occasions.

So which one should you drink? The vast majority of wine writers rate Louis Roederer as the number one non-vintage champagne—it constantly tops blind tastings and was many an expert's recommendation as the best way to bring in the new millennium. Connoisseurs rave about its tiny, perfectly formed bubbles and clean taste, which has a creamy, buttery finish. Then there's the smell—a mix of toasted brioche and honey (many good champagnes have a distinct biscuity taste), combined with the scent of berries thanks to the profusion of pinot noir grapes—the proportion is roughly two to one pinot noir to chardonnay. Louis Roederer is also aged in wood, which is something of a rarity—most non-vintage champagnes are aged in stainless steel or glass containers—and comes from the same producer as the much more bling Cristal. Indeed, Cristal would have been number one if it wasn't so darned expensive—and its image wasn't so trashy, a problem its producers are well aware of. Brut Premier, on the other hand, is classy and accessible.

Cristal

The best way to get your kick from champagne? Serve it at 45°F (any warmer, and the contents will foam excessively) from a flute glass that will preserve the bubbles.

CRISTAL

Where? Good wine merchants • www.cellarbrokers.com

How much? From $170–$400 per bottle, depending on vintage

P. Diddy famously spent $216,000 on Cristal in a London club—not as hard as you'd imagine when you consider the price. A cult name for quality quaffing.

KRUG GRAND CUVÉE

Where? www.winebuyer.com • www.internetwines.com • Morrell Wines, One Rockefeller Plaza, N.Y.C. • all good wine merchants

How much? $150–$299

Dating back to 1843, this champagne house offers no entry-level bottles. "We start where others stop," they claim. Krug also has a distinctive taste: slightly dusty with hints of dried fruit, toasted brioche, roses, and violets, a unique bouquet that's said to be the result of storing champagne in oak barrels.

Krug Grand Cuvée

PARLEZ-VOUS CHAMPAGNE?

Deciphering the label on a champagne bottle can be a perplexing experience, especially when the words are in French, and when "extra dry" is not as dry as "Brut" (meaning "dry"). Confusing. Below is a brief guide to some key terms.

- **Blanc de blanc**: Champagne made using only white grapes, usually chardonnay. This is a classic aperitif champagne.
- **Blanc de noir**: Champagne made using black grapes, usually pinot noir; it tastes particularly good with food.
- **Brut**: Dry.
- **Brut nature**: Bone dry.
- **Cuvée**: Blend.
- **Cru**: Literally "growth." This also refers to the villages in the Champagne region that provide wines of exceptional quality.
- **Extra dry**: Not as dry as brut; a slight sweetness.
- **Grand cru**: "Great growth." This phrase is attributed to a vineyard with the very highest rating and also identifies the Champagne villages that produce the very best wine—17 have been bestowed this status.
- **Grand marque**: A group of the biggest and most famous champagne names.
- **Mise en cave** (followed by date): The date the wine was cellared.
- **Non-vintage** (NV): A champagne mostly from a single year, but with older wines blended in. This is the most common form of champagne.
- **Premier cru**: A vineyard with the second highest rating.
- **Prestige cuvée**: A champagne house's most expensive champagne; some are vintage, others non-vintage.
- **Récoltant-manipulant (RM)**: An independent grower-producer; so not one of the grandes marques.
- **Vintage**: Champagne of a single, notably good year—1990 and 1996 are considered the two best.

Chocolate

L'Artisan du Chocolat

Where?
89 Lower Sloane St., London SW1 •
www.artisanduchocolat.com

How much?
Sampler boxes $7–$170

L'Artisan du Chocolat

Multi-Michelin-starred chef Gordon Ramsay describes L'Artisan du Chocolat as "the Bentley of chocolate" and theirs is the only range he will serve in his restaurants. Ditto Heston Blumenthal, owner of The Fat Duck, "The Best Restaurant in the World," according to *Restaurant* magazine. All of which is praise indeed, especially for such a young company (it has only been running since 1999)—and a British one, at that.

Traditionally, the world's best chocolatiers have been confined to Belgium, Switzerland and France. The ambitious aim of the co-founder, Gerard Coleman, is to make L'Artisan du Chocolat the best in the world, while ensuring that quality is never, ever compromised; hence the company has no immediate plans for expansion. Indeed, the self-confessed perfectionist is behind the manufacture of every single chocolate and the company, like the ever-innovative Blumenthal, is known for its use of unusual ingredients—flavors include sesame, Bramley apple, green cardamom and tobacco. Banana and thyme is its bestseller, a thin shell of intense chocolate encasing two very different flavors that somehow balance each other magnificently.

Coleman believes his fans "are more open to experimentation than the French, Belgians or Germans, who have more defined tastes and don't want you to start putting cardamom in their chocolate." Coleman, himself a chef by training, spent time working with esteemed Belgian chocolate company Pierre Marcolini before branching out on his own. Each of his chocolates is freshly made and, once bought, should be stored in a cool place and eaten within a couple of weeks. Unlike most chocolatiers, who only use one bean, Coleman uses different beans to complement the different flavors of the centres, all of which are made using the finest raw ingredients. As well as taste, Coleman is also obsessed with texture—be it the crunch of a nutty praline or the silky smoothness of a berry filling—believing this to be another crucial factor in the making of perfect chocolate.

PIERRE MARCOLINI

Where? 485 Park Ave., N.Y.C • 212.755.5150 • www.marcolinichocolatier.com

How much? Boxed selections $18–$285

This Belgian chocolatier has been in business since 1990 and is one of the few who still processes all of his own cocoa beans—according to Belgian law, only producers who make their wares from scratch can technically call themselves "chocolatiers." He now has shops in London and Tokyo. Bestsellers include his praline, the orange-thyme combination a particular favorite.

LA MAISON DU CHOCOLAT

Where? 225 Rue de Faubourg de St. Honore, Paris • 30 Rockefeller Center and 1018 Madison Ave., N.Y.C., plus other boutiques in Paris, N.Y.C., London, and Tokyo • www.lamaisonduchocolat.com

How much? Boxed samples $7–$97

Robert Linxe of the Paris-based La Maison du Chocolat is known in the industry as "the creator" and the original superstar chocolatier. He is obsessed with ganache, a gooey centre that is made from cream and chocolate, sometimes adding an infusion. The Bacchus truffle with rum and raisin filling is his self-confessed favorite; each raisin is "tailed and flamed" before being impregnated with a rum vapor.

La Maison du Chocolat

Claret / Bordeaux

Château Mouton Rothschild, 1945

Where?

Acker Merrall and Condit, 160 W. 72 St., N.Y.C •
212.787.1700 • www.ackerwines.com

Wine Bid • www.winebid.com

The Chicago Wine Company, 5663 W. Howard St., Niles, IL •
847.647.8789 • www.tcwc.com

How much?

$4,500 per bottle and up, up! • Other vintages start at
around $140

Château
Mouton
Rothschild

How much is a bottle of the best red wine? How much are you willing to pay? Even the top wine cellers do not have cases and cases of Chateau Mouton Rothschild, 1945, lying around. Rather, this is a wine that will occasionally come up for auction, and if you care to sample the very best you must keep abreast.

Despite claims to the contrary, there have only been three great red Bordeaux vintages since the Second World War—1945, 1961, and 1982. Of course, one never knows a truly great vintage until several years down the line, so when it comes to buying claret it is worth taking risks.

Nowadays, more people than ever are interested in expensive wine, thanks in part to the influential wine critic Robert Parker and his "100-point" system, but also because of the burgeoning economies of China and Russia. Blue-chip chateaux still attract the most interest: think Château Lafite Rothschild, Château Latour or Château d'Yquem, which is famous for holding back some supplies for later sales. All are names worth noting when purchasing Bordeaux.

But what's the best? The answer, of course, is totally subjective—one man's Château Latour is another man's Ribena—but the respected wine magazine *Decanter* recently came up with a suggestion: Château Mouton Rothschild, 1945, the one wine their critics claimed everyone should "drink before they die."

The magazine described it as "intense, concentrated, indescribable… without doubt the greatest claret of the 20th century." Not bad for a château that only officially received "Première Cru Classe" (the highest classification possible) in 1973. The château lies opposite Lafite and has been growing vines since the 1720s. Mouton Rothschild's *terroir*, or soil, is formed of deep gravel beds with a subsoil consisting of clay and limestone. Their claret is made up of 85 per cent cabernet sauvignon, 10 per cent cabernet franc, and five per cent merlot. Oenophiles can tour the château, taking in the original artwork by Picasso, but the cellar, which houses 35,000 bottles of untouched wine, some dating back to 1859, is strictly off-limits.

Incidentally, a tip for cheaper claret—and indeed red wine in general—is to decant it into a glass vessel before drinking. This will add oxygen, instantly making the most bog-standard bottle taste like a million dollars. A similar trick can be done with white using a ceramic jug to keep it cooler.

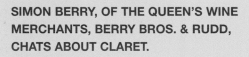

Château Cheval Blanc

CHÂTEAU PETRUS

Where? Fine wine shops nationwide

How much? From approximately $70

A Merlot-dominated claret that has risen to prominence, in part because Robert Parker is such a fan.

CHÂTEAU CHEVAL BLANC

Where? Fine wine shops nationwide

How much? From approximately $80

A wine that's found fame for a very different reason—it's featured in the acclaimed movie *Sideways*. According to Miles, the film's anti-hero, this is "the only wine worthy of seducing a woman." It has an unusually high percentage of cabernet franc grapes, which doesn't usually produce good wines on its own, except in the case of Château Cheval Blanc. The result is a lush, velvety texture with a slight truffle and mushroom tinge on the tongue. Unlike most clarets, you can drink this one relatively young—after seven or eight years—but ideally wait until it's around 20 years old. Ignore Miles when it comes to vintage, though; despite his claims to 1961, the ultimate is actually 1947. Parker gave this one 100 out of 100.

SIMON BERRY, OF THE QUEEN'S WINE MERCHANTS, BERRY BROS. & RUDD, CHATS ABOUT CLARET.

What makes claret so great?

Simon Berry: "It's unique. Cabernet sauvignon is grown throughout the world, but the finest clarets are still the greatest wines in that they are never bettered. You might have to pay anything over £50 ($90) a bottle to get something fantastic—but with tickets to football matches costing that nowadays, it's not a lot for one of life's great luxuries."

How should the perfect glass of claret taste?

SB: "Almost indescribable—but with an extraordinary balance of fruit, acidity, and density. It will have great complexity—a taste that changes and develops over time—and will linger in the mouth for a significant period. It's instantly recognizable, though, once you've experienced a few."

What are good, more affordable options?

SB: "The 1990s and 1989s are wonderful now. And great properties from 1997 are very affordable."

For the first-time buyer, what advice would you give?

SB: "Find a good wine merchant—someone who you trust, and who will take you through what will end up as a journey of discovery. And remember that it's all about personal taste. Really, the only important question is: is it good to drink?"

Coffee

Kopi Luwak

Where?
www.indonesiangrocery.com • www.animalcoffee.com

How much?
From $30 for 2 ounces to $180 per pound, depending on bean and place of purchase

A good cup of coffee should be treated in the same manner as a fine wine—sniffed, savored and respected. The best blend is down to personal taste, but the most expensive—and the most rare—is that ground from the kopi luwak. These beans (*Robusta* or *Arabica*) from Indonesia are produced in the most unusual way: from the excrement of civets who feast on coffee cherries, eating them whole, bean and all. When they have passed through their bodies, the bean remains, albeit covered in a parchment-like layer. The beans are then collected by locals, who remove the shell and sell them on.

The result, thanks to the civet's gastric juices, is a uniquely smooth flavor that many describe as reminiscent of caramel and chocolate without any hint of bitterness. Customers include Damian Hirst.

Civet Coffee, Kopi Luwak

JAMAICAN BLUE MOUNTAIN
Where? gourmet shops • www.jablum.us •
Canada: www.goldstarcoffee.com
How much? From $32 per pound
With the exception of the Kopi Luwak, Blue Mountain is the coffee synonymous with high prices. This is because the beans are so hard to reach—they grow 6,900 feet above sea-level in Jamaica's Blue Mountains. The result is a sweet, full-bodied cup.

PEET'S
Where? Peet's coffee shops in San Francisco Bay Area • Peet's in Santa Monica • Peet's Coffee and Tea, 3401 Fremont Ave. N., Seattle • Peet's, 100 Mount Auburn, Boston • Scharffen Berger, 473 Amsterdam Ave., N.Y.C. • www.peets.com
How much? From $14 for 12oz
American coffee lovers happily pay for Peet's, a boutique coffee from Emeryville, CA, that's best known in the Bay Area. Enough said.

Ice Cream

Corrado Costanzo

Where?
Via Spaventa 7, Noto, Sicily
How much?
Prices from $2/€1.40 a scoop

Anyone with a sweet tooth should get the next flight to Sicily—where they even eat ice cream for breakfast in the form of a hollowed-out brioche filled with *gelato*. Ice cream may have been invented here around the 8th century, when Arabs inhabiting Sicily first thought to scoop the ice from the slopes of Mount Etna, and combine it with sugar, milk, and local flavors, such as oranges, lemons, almonds, and roses.

The best gelato comes from the town of Noto in the south of the island. Here you'll find the world's most mouthwatering scoops at Corrado Costanzo, a *gelateria* that has been running for almost 50 years. Along with the more traditional flavors are more unusual concoctions made from mulberry, rose, and jasmine. Costanzo is fastidious about preparing his puddings with the very best local ingredients, only using flowers picked in the evening when they are at their most fragrant.

The bestseller, though, is *granita al mandarino*, a sorbet made with the juiciest local mandarin

Gelato

oranges, the epitome of refreshing zinginess, and not in the least bit tart. People will travel continents to sample what Costanzo calls "the taste of Sicily in your mouth." Of course this is not strictly an ice cream—but then neither is gelato (italian ice cream), which is made using milk rather than cream.

IL LABORATORIO DEL GELATO
Where? 95 Orchard St., N.Y.C. • 212.343.9922 • www.labortoriodelgelato.com
How much? Single two-flavor serving, $3.25, $8.25 per pint
Jon Snyder, a one time stock trader, who became a gelato master during his Ciao Bello days, offers 200 flavors at this Manhatten Lower East Side storefront. Among them are nine intense chocolates and such originals as Black Sesame and Honey Lavendar.

MARGIE'S CANDIES
Where? 1960 N. Western Ave., Chicago • 773.384.1035
How much? Spectacular sundaes from $4

The best ice cream concoctions in America, according to Michael Turback, author of *More Than A Month of Sundaes*. Margie's treats have been enjoyed by everyone from Al Capone to the Beatles. Go for the Atomic Hot Fudge.

SERENDIPITY 3
Where? 225 E. 60th St., N.Y.C. • 212.838.3531
How much? $8.50–$20
This ice cream parlor/antiques shop has one ice cream dish worth ordering: the Bipolar Frrrozen Hot Chocolate. You must also consider its Strawberry Fields Sundae (the secret is in the cheesecake), the all-American Maple Walnut Sundae, and, of course, the Outrageous Banana Split.

THE GLOBETROTTING GELATO-ITE

Wherever you are in the world, it's good to know that a decent scoop of vanilla is close at hand. Below is a guide for the globetrotting gelato-ite:

Giolitti
After Sicily, Rome is the best place in Italy to find ice cream. This atmospheric café has been going since 1900 and serves some of the most heavenly scoops around.
Via Uffici del Vicario 40, Rome, Italy

Gelatauro
Since Bologna is the gastronomic heart of Italy, the locals are extremely fussy when it comes to their treats. The locals decree this place the best for mind-blowing ice cream.
Via San Vitale 90, Bologna, Italy

Persicco
Due to its Italian heritage, Argentine helado is some of the best in the world. Persicco is the leading up-market chain, thanks to its all-natural ingredients.
Migueletes 886, Palermo, Buenos Aires, Argentina, plus branches

Berthillon
If too many patisserie delicacies are weighing you down, this is widely regarded as the best ice cream in France.
31 Rue St.-Louis-en-L'Ile, Paris, France

Alba Gold
Alba Gold, a proper Italian artisan ice cream, is only available in small quantities since most is sold directly to London's Michelin-starred restaurants. The company's ingredients are the finest available: pistachios from Sicily, for instance, or sun-matured strawberries from Morocco. The tiramisu flavor is exceptional.
72 High St., London W3

Morelli's in Harrods
The outpost of the Broadstairs branch offers a bespoke ice cream service in Harrods' famous food hall. The helpful staff will try to accommodate all tastes—requested flavors have included "baked beans on toast" and "pickled onions."
87-135 Brompton Rd., London SW1

Coppelia Calle
Havana's infamous ice cream parlor was built as the Revolution's 'gift to the people'. Tourists are guided to a separate outdoor kiosk, but should sneak a look at the futuristic interior of the main 1966 building. In true Socialist style, choices are limited to vanilla, chocolate and caramel.
23 between Calle L and the Malecon, Havana, Cuba

Yolato
Yummy Yolato is frozen yoghurt made gelato-style. Both delicious and quite possibly healthy, you can buy take-out cones, cups or pints at five Yolato locations in Manhattan and two in New Jersey (Edgewater and Paramus). Visit www.yolato.com to find new stands.

Olive oil

Manni Per Me

Manni
Per Me

Where?

www.buymanni.com

How much?

about $35 for a 3½oz bottle

There's everyday olive oil—the kind you use for cooking—and then there's the special stuff, the gourmet liquid gold reserved for drizzling, dipping, and savoring. Manni Per Me is officially the world's most expensive oil olive, but, for once, the eyebrow-raising prices are in sync with quality, as this is also the world's very best.

The oil was created in 2000, when Italian filmmaker Armando Manni became a father for the first time and wanted to find the purest olive oil possible for his son. For this he needed science and enlisted the help of the University of Florence. Scientists there pinpointed the exact time the olives should be picked, when they would be at their richest in antioxidants and they would also have the fullest flavor. Manni bought some groves on Mount Amiata in southern Tuscany and put the research into practice.

The result of all this careful planning is two oils. *Per Mio Figlio* (for my child) is ideal for babies and young children—Madonna uses it for Rocco and Lourdes—and has a smooth, buttery taste. *Per Me* (for me) is for adults and has a full-flavored and peppery taste. It's so rich, in fact, that enthusiasts claim you can use less oil than you normally would—which is one way to save money. Incidentally, the difference in taste between the two oils is because olives from higher up the mountain are used for *Per Me* as these have a more intense flavor. Production is limited to 550 gallons a year. The oil can only be purchased over the internet and is sent out in special temperature-controlled containers.

Per Me is used in such snazzy restaurants as Eve's in Alexandria, VA, Spiagga in Chicago, and Heidi's in Minneapolis. It is also used in Les Ambassadeurs at the Hôtel de Crillon in Paris, in Jean-Georges Vongerichten's top New York restaurants, and in the Park Hyatt in Tokyo.

Chefs shout Manni's praise from the roofs of their Michelin-starred restaurants. "It's a rare breed of person who strives for perfection in his chosen line of work," says Thomas Keller of the French Laundry in Napa Valley, Per se in New York and Bouchon in Las Vegas, "Armando Manni personifies this determination—he has successfully produced the best and healthiest extra virgin olive oil on the market."

"When I first tasted Manni's oils, I knew I had tasted something amazing."

Jean-Georges Vongerichten of Vong and the Mercer Kitchen in New York

CASA PONS MAS PORTELL

Where? www.earthy.com
How much? $24.50 for 16oz, organic: $27.50

Spain is the biggest producer of olive oil in the world—it has around 370 million olive trees—and certain oil snobs prefer fruitier Spanish oils to Italian varieties. Pons, which has an almost almondy taste, is one of the best. All the olives are hand-picked, and the oil is made in a traditional stone mill in Catalonia. Each bottle is individually numbered.

NICOLAS ALZIARI

Where? Citarella stores in N.Y.C. and Easthampton, N.Y. • www.citarella.com • www.hypergourmet.com
How much? 1 liter U.S.$40/Can$55

Few visitors leave Nice without buying this oil in its distinctive blue and yellow tin. Alziari uses small black olives crushed on a millstone that was powered by the neighboring river until relatively recently. The resulting taste is gorgeously buttery. Use this to make the perfect salade niçoise.

Nicolas Alziari

A BRIEF GLOSSARY OF OLIVE OIL TERMS

Understanding the wording on a bottle of olive oil is a little like deciphering a bottle of wine—although it should be noted that, unlike wine, olive oil does not improve with age; instead it has a shelf life of about a year. The best are sold in colored glass bottles, as light and heat can be harmful to the oil. Greener olive oils are made using olives earlier in the season—because they're not as juicy as when they are ripe, this type uses up more olives and is therefore more expensive.

- **Single estate**: From a single family business or farm. Two of the best in Tuscany are Capezzana and Badia a Coltibuono.
- **Blended**: An oil made using olives from different estates, varieties, regions, sometimes even countries.
- **First cold press**: Oil from the first pressing of the olives, with no applied heat.
- **Extra virgin olive oil**: Production is by hand or machine and no chemicals are used. This will have no more than one per cent acidity resulting in a fantastic aroma and flavor.
- **Virgin olive oil**: As above, but with an acidity of up to two percent.
- **Olive oil**: Has up to 3.3 per cent acidity. This is a lower quality since it's a blend of virgin olive oil and refined (oil that has been chemically treated to neutralize strong tastes). The most common olive oil.
- **Unfiltered**: Contains small bits of olive; will have lots of flavor but sediment at the bottom.

Spice

MM Spices

Where?
M/S Mahesh Kumar Mohan Das,
Shop No 206/3, Clock Tower,
Jodhpur, India

How much?
From $2

MM Spices

India is the motherland of spice—venture into any market and you can smell the spice-sellers selling sachets from hessian sacks a mile off. The only problem is the bewildering array before you, coupled with merchants understandably unused to dealing with curious foreigners.

Which is where MM Spices comes in. The Jodhpur shop, close to the main square, is both accessible and fun. It even has celebrity endorsement—the actor Jeremy Irons often visits Jodhpur for antiques, the other ware for which the city is famous, and will pop here for some seasoning. Plus the proprietor, King Rose, is one shopkeeper you won't forget in a hurry. This self-styled Bollywood hero, complete with medallion, moustache, and a pair of jeans that leaves nothing to the imagination, is the ultimate salesman. The result? It's virtually impossible to leave empty-handed.

Luckily, this is one of the best spice shops in India and sells its stock to restaurants nationwide. King Rose sits customers down on a plastic stool and propels them into sensory overload, encouraging them to smell, taste, and touch his entire stock, from powdered turmeric, saffron, cinnamon bark, and a million varieties of tea, to the "winter tonic," a sort of natural viagra for men.

Amateur cooks can pick up bags of masala, a blend of different spices, for about 250 rupees ($6), including an easy recipe for making the most out-of-this-world curry. All this *and* a drawstring silk bag to carry home your wares.

HERBORISTERIE AVENZOAR
Where? 78 Bis Derb N'Khel, Rahba Lakdima, Marrakech, Morocco
How much? From $2
The world's other great spice center is Morocco. In Marrakech, ask your guide to direct you toward Herboristerie Avenzoar for good-quality spices, as well as relaxing massages using different plant oils.

THE SPICE HOUSE
Where? 1512 N. Wells St., Chicago • 312.274.0378 • outlets also in Evanston, IL and Milwaukee, WI • www.thespicehouse.com.
How much? From $2
There are good spice markets in other North American cities, but The Spice House has an extraordinary array of aromatic spices, its salespeople are knowledgable and one can order online.

Tea

Silver Needles

Where?
Various specialist teashops and tea websites, including:
www.theteatable.com and www.tentea.com •
Claridge's tearoom, Brook St., London W1

How much?
$7.50 per 1oz to $22 per 4oz

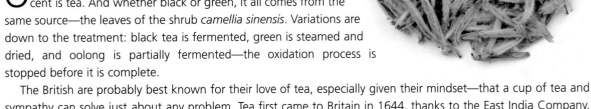

Silver Needles tea

Of all liquids consumed by the world's population, 40 per cent is tea. And whether black or green, it all comes from the same source—the leaves of the shrub *camellia sinensis*. Variations are down to the treatment: black tea is fermented, green is steamed and dried, and oolong is partially fermented—the oxidation process is stopped before it is complete.

The British are probably best known for their love of tea, especially given their mindset—that a cup of tea and sympathy can solve just about any problem. Tea first came to Britain in 1644, thanks to the East India Company, and by the 18th century it had become the country's most popular beverage. So much so that following the Boston Tea Party, patriotic Americans showed their allegiance to their country by swapping tea-drinking for coffee.

For a really special brew, connoisseurs should try Silver Needles, one of the rarest teas—and therefore one of the most expensive. It is also a white tea, a type that has become increasingly popular in recent years due to the fact that it's packed full of antioxidants—up to three times more than green, in fact.

White tea is made from immature tea leaves that must be picked before the buds are fully opened. Silver Needles comes from the Fujian Province of China and is picked within a two-day period in early spring. The tea gets its name from the dried leaves, which are needle-shaped and silver in color due to the fuzz that still covers the bud. The result is a tea admired for its full-bodied and exceptionally delicate flavor.

Once the preserve of the Chinese Emperor and *nobody* else—900 years ago, during the Song Dynasty, a cup of this tea would have cost you your head—it is now readily available over the internet.

FORTNUM & MASON
Where? 181 Piccadilly, London W1
How much? From £7/$12 for a 250g (8oz) tin
The upmarket grocer has a rare tea bar that sells one of the best selections of uncommon teas in the world. Popular varieties include rose pouchong, Russian caravan, and Margaret's Hope.

MARIAGE FRÈRES
Where? 30 Rue du Bourg-Tibourg, Paris • www.mariagefreres.com
How much? $144/€120 per 100g (3½oz)
Another excellent purveyor of tea is Mariage Frères, a Parisian company that sells over 50 types of Darjeeling. Brumes d'Himalaya ("Himalayan mists") is their most expensive; the leaf tips are picked from the "first flush" (i.e. the first spring harvest) at a single estate in Darjeeling. Incidentally, most "Darjeeling" sold in shops is nothing of the kind, since it comes from Kenya or Sri Lanka. Beware of imitations.

Vodka

Jean-Marc XO

Jean-Marc XO

Where?
www.winexwine.com • Good liquor stores
How much?
From $58

Russian, Swedish, Polish—which vodka is the best? French, actually. Jean-Marc XO has none of the vodka "afterburn" (the feeling as the liquid travels down the throat) that's so familiar with many Eastern European brands. This is because it is made in the same manner as cognac (hence the "XO"). Indeed, the brand recently won a prestigious taste test when the U.S. Beverage Tasting Institute rated it the best vodka ever, with a score of 96 out of 100.

The company was started by Jean-Marc Daucourt, a French distiller from Cognac. "Vodka isn't big in France," he explains, "but I discovered it 20 years ago when I lived in America, and knew that we could do better."

Using the same copper stills that are used in the cognac-making process, the vodka is distilled nine times to remove all the impurities—most vodkas are distilled twice at the most—then micro-oxygenated to further kill the afterburn. Jean-Marc Daucourt is the only company in the world that does this. The result is the perfect vodka—clear, with floral notes, anise, and a pleasingly powdery feel in the mouth. Best of all, it doesn't taste too alcoholic—it's as odorless and as flavorless as it gets, the way vodka ought to be. In fact, you can merrily drink Jean-Marc XO on the rocks without wincing.

GREY GOOSE

Where? Good liquor stores
How much? About $35
The world's most popular super-premium brand is also blended and bottled in Cognac. The making of the company was winning a taste test in 1998—the same one Jean-Marc XO pipped them to more recently. A favorite with many top mixologists, Grey Goose has a creamy taste and is widely available.

BELVEDERE

Where? Good liquor stores
How much? About $35
Another popular super-premium brand, Belvedere is made in Poland from rye (most Polish vodka comes from potatoes). The taste is creamy with hints of vanilla, and is the bling vodka choice—a long-standing favorite with the hip-hop community.

Health & beauty

"The best thing is to look natural, but it takes a lot of makeup to look natural."

Calvin Klein

Aftershave

Creed Green Irish Tweed

Where?
38 Avenue Pierre 1er de Serbie, Paris • Neiman Marcus, Bergdorf Goodman, and other better department stores • www.overstockperfume.com

How much?
From $140

Green Irish Tweed is Creed's bestselling fragrance for gentlemen—that is Gentlemen with a capital G. The aftershave was originally created for none other than Cary Grant. Wearers today are just as suave: George Clooney, Pierce Brosnan, Robbie Williams, David Beckham—even Prince Charles is a fan.

Part of Green Irish Tweed's charm is the way it smells so light—there's no overpowering afterburn here. The balanced blend of floral, green, and woody notes include verbena, violet leaves, Florentine iris, sandalwood, and ambergris. It could be said that Creed started the current trend for bespoke scents, as all but two of their fragrances were originally made exclusively for their wearers. Spring Flowers, for instance, was created for Audrey Hepburn, while Madonna has spent thousands and waited three years for Creed to make her own couture scent, a process that is based on the wearer's personality, passions, and olfactory preferences. Creed, established in 1760, is one of only a handful of perfume houses still privately owned. The current owner, Oliver Creed, is something of a scent obsessive, sourcing the purest essence of rose from Bulgaria and Morocco, jasmine and irises from Italy, tuberose from India, and genuine Parma violets. The most expensive of these is the Bulgarian rose, which costs $50,000 to $80,000 for 2lbs.

Creed Green Irish Tweed

Creed still makes all of its perfumes using the traditional infusion technique. The components are weighed, mixed and filtered by hand, then left to seep for weeks, while Oliver tinkers to make each batch perfect. The oils used are always slightly different, which means that the scents vary in fragrance year on year, rather like a fine wine. Experts claim you can instantly distinguish a Creed fragrance, as their scents are notably deeper, richer, and more eccentric than any others. In fact, many Creed scents are initially rejected by department store buyers for smelling too unusual. To appreciate Creed, it would seem, takes time, as most of the rejected fragrances end up bestsellers. Creed also takes a deep pocket—developing a passion for their fragrances is an expensive habit, but, given the company of their wearers, it is well worth it.

PARFUMS DE NICOLAI NEW YORK

Where? www.beautyhabit.com
How much? $80

Made by Patricia de Nicolai, the granddaughter of Pierre Guerlain, the esteemed nose Dr Luca Turin describes this, one of his favorite aftershaves, as "more a companion for life than a mere perfume, a hugely complex and exquisitely balanced citrus-warm composition that never shouts but glows mysteriously at close range." Indeed the spicy scent, the ingredients of which include bergamot, cloves, amber, and vetiver, is highly coveted by knowledgeable cologne-lovers. Quite an achievement given that Parfums de Nicolai receives scant publicity.

CHRISTIAN DIOR EAU SAVAGE

Where? All good perfume shops and department stores
How much? Prices from $40

Famous for its archetypal "aftershavey" smell—described by some as "the very essence of a man"—this was actually the first mass-marketed scent also used by women. Eau Savage was created in 1966, and remains a bestseller. A classic that stands the test of time.

Parfums de Nicolai New York

What every gentleman should have in his bathroom cabinet

In the first instance a gentleman should think English. D. R. Harris & Co. (www.drharris.co.uk) of St James's is widely regarded as having the best shaving soap—opt for almond—while Geo. F. Trumper (www.trumpers.com), the Mayfair barbers founded in 1875, has what must be one of the largest selections of razors in the world. For a steady shave try the Warwick, an Edwardian-style razor available with a Gillette Mach-3 blade fitting, which is the best blade.

For the perfect shaving brush, what about one made of pure silver-tip badger from brush experts Kent (www.kentbrushes.com)? Or maybe try Czech & Speake (www.czechspeake.com), or Truefitt & Hill (www.truefitt-tandhill.com). The ultimate shaving oil, which is much more efficient than foam or gel, isn't quite so exclusive. King of Shaves is recommended by all the best barbers, even the most traditional, and is available at all good pharmacies.

Bronzer

St Tropez Shimmering Bronzing Mist

St Tropez Shimmering Bronzing Mist

Where?

Sephora, Victoria's Secrets, day spas, etc.

How much?

$26

Despite the fact that we're all more wary of sun-exposure than ever before, due to side effects that range from ageing of the skin to melanoma, the desire for a tan refuses to fade. In fact, looking lean and bronzed is a must for modern celebrities and civilians alike. It's best to go to a salon and have fake tan applied by a professional, but if you're short on time and cash, and prepared to do it yourself, the best product you can use is St Tropez's Shimmering Bronzing Mist. This recent innovation comes from the originators of the truly realistic fake tan, and is a consistent favorite with beauty editors and celebs thanks to the three-dimensional sheen, which reflects light and helps make the tan appear deeper and more authentic. It dries quickly, but be warned—you'll need to cover the bathroom floor before applying. This can be a messy little number.

Clarins Self Tanning Instant Gel

CLARINS SELF TANNING INSTANT GEL

Where? Clarins shops • department stores

How much? $30

A light transparent gel that's easy to apply—it glides quickly and fluidly over the body and develops into a natural healthy tan within a couple of hours.

LANCÔME FLASH BRONZER AIRBRUSH

Where? Lancôme stores in N.Y.C., Short Hills, Dallas, Brea, Santa Clara • Department stores worldwide

How much? $28

This spray bronzer, raved about by Jessica Simpson and Kylie Minogue, is extremely easy to use: just angle it a few inches from the body and spray away. The very fine mist coats every millimetre of skin and is absorbed easily. Best of all, a natural colour will develop within a couple of hours.

BRILLIANT BRONZERS FOR THE FACE

There's a difference between bronzers for the body and those for the face: the latter should be more sensitive and moisturizing. The best of them all is Sisley's Self Tanning Gel (www.sisley-cosmetics.com), which develops a natural tan within a couple of hours of being applied (available at Bergdorf Goodman in New York, Holt Renfrew in Toronto), while Helena Rubenstein's glitter-tinged Golden Beauty Sun Tan Express gel comes in a close second (www.helenarubinstein.com). We also rate Lancome's Flash Bronzer with vitamin E for sheer ease and value for money (www.lancome.com), and Fake Bake's "The Face," which includes peptides to help prevent those pesky wrinkles (www.fakebake.net).

Bubble bath

Laura Mercier Crème Brûlée Honey Bath

Where?
www.lauramercier.com • Department stores worldwide

How much?
$40

Laura Mercier Crème Brûlée Honey Bath

As the poet, Sylvia Plath, once said: "There must be quite a few things that a bath won't cure, but I don't know many of them." A long, hot soak is the most indulgent and effective way to unwind after a hard day. Happily, the days when a scoop of bath salts and a bar of cold cream soap would suffice are long gone. Instead, it's now possible to recreate the luxury of a day spa in your own bathroom. A tricky and potentially messy process, but if there's a product that helps you achieve this in one easy step, it's Laura Mercier's Crème Brûlée Honey Bath. With a silky texture and a heavenly, sweet-honey scent that seems good enough to eat, this product creates the finest bubbly bubbles going. Thoroughly luxurious and one of the nicest gifts a girl can give—or receive.

E. COUDRAY JACINTHE AND ROSE BATH CRÈME

Where? L.T. Piver, 152 Rue Gallieni, 92100, Boulogne, France • Parfume Shoppe, 226–757 W. Hastings St., Vancouver, BC., Canada • www.coudray-parfumeur.com • Department stores worldwide

How much? $25

In 1822, during the reign of Louis XVIII, a doctor-chemist named Edmond Coudray started to supply soaps and salves from France to European royalty. Later, this creamy bubble bath became the brand's best-seller. What makes this bubble bath so great is its blancmange-like texture, making it a pleasure to plunge one's hands into before rinsing off under running bathwater. Irresistible.

ROSE & CO. APOTHECARY ROSE PETAL BATH AND SHOWER CRÈME

Where? 84 Main St., Haworth, West Yorkshire • www.rose-apothecary.co.uk

How much? £8/$14

This gorgeous smelling Yorkshire brand originates from the romantic village of Howarth, once the home of the Brontë sisters and still home to Rose & Co. Apothecary—a shop full of dusty glass cabinets and botanical concoctions. This lavish bubble bath is spiked with pure oil of roses and is mild, gentle, and addictively sweet-but-tart. Use it once and you'll be a convert for life.

Rose & Co. Apothecary Rose Petal Bath and Shower Crème

Compact

Givenchy Prisme

Where?
www.givenchy.com • Department stores • Sephora
How much?
$43/€32

One of the most practical, pretty, and glamorous make-up items a girl can have, a good compact is a handbag necessity, and a quality mirrored style is a prized accessory that will last a lifetime.

Founded by Hubert de Givenchy in 1957, Parfums Givenchy was an instant hit, becoming one of the most desirable beauty brands in the world, thanks, no doubt, to the brand's associations with screen icon of the day, Audrey Hepburn. The French company has maintained its chic image with exquisite offerings, such as the Prisme pressed powder quartet, which allows the user to blend together a perfect shade to match the required skin tone. Available in nine different shades from a beautiful pastel white to "Impertinent Rose" and "Cool Beige," its angular, black-lacquer packaging makes it one of the most beautifully designed compacts around.

Givenchy Prisme

Chantecaille

CHANTECAILLE
Where? www.eluxury.com • Department stores worldwide
How much? About $60 and up
French-born, U.S.-based Sylvie Chanticaille, the former force behind Prescriptives, has created some of the best foundations and powders in the world. Her finely textured compact make-up powder foundation, presented in a galvanized nickel container, is one of the best compacts on the market. The pale shades are particularly strong and an excellent option for those with fairer skins. Available in eight shades, including shell, camel, and peach.

SHU UEMURA
Shu Uemura

Where? Shu Uemura in Vancouver, San Fransisco, Costa Mesa, N.Y.C., Boston and cosmetic counters elsewhere
How much? About $12 for compact, $32 for powder
This forward-thinking Japanese powder has a subtly reflective finish that eliminates shine. We also love the packaging.

And the best loose powder...

With a delicate gold shimmer, **T. Le Clerc's classic Banane Powder** is the legendary loose powder. It was first created in 1881 and is a fine, soft powder that achieves an instant matt finish once applied over foundation. Make-up artists adore the stuff, as does a host of celebrities, including Madonna, Jennifer Aniston and Drew Barrymore.

Face cream

La Prairie Skin Caviar Luxe Cream

Where?
Top cosmetic counters in North America
and elsewhere • www.laprairie.com •
www.makemeheal.com
How much?
From $325

It's a million-dollar question in a billion-dollar industry—what's the best face cream in the world? Skins vary as much as body shape, hair texture, and coloring. There are thousands of creams, ranging from ultra-cheap (see p.64) to expensive and exclusive emollients to cater for this huge market, so pinpointing just one is practically impossible. According to recent scientific research, venix, the gunky white stuff that covers newborn babies, is apparently the best moisturizer in the world. Eeew. And yes, scientists are working out how they can recreate this and sell it in a jar. But in the meantime, we'll have to make do with good old-fashioned cream moisturizers, and if we had to pick the best all-round effective one, something that glides on beautifully and sinks in without the oil-slick effect, it would have to be La Prairie's Skin Caviar Luxe.

*Natura Bissé
Diamond Cream*

It's not just the expensive-looking blue glass tub and silver spoon that replicates a real caviar spoon—although that's a bonus—or the fact that the Beckhams both use it, this legendary moisturizer actually delivers results. Rich in caviar extract, which is known for its nourishing properties, it is light but rich and sinks in effortlessly. If you could only own one face cream in the world, perhaps this should be it.

*La Prairie Skin
Caviar Luxe Cream*

NATURA BISSÉ DIAMOND CREAM
Where? www.visagebeauty.com • Neiman Marcus, Barneys, Stonewater
How much? $270
The silver jar looks expensive and appeals to the inner J-Lo in us all, but it's the cream inside that's valuable. Just one application and you know this is special, as it sinks deeply into the skin. OK, so it doesn't contain diamonds: instead, the potent ingredients are straight from the sea. It's also packed with grapeseed extract, beta-glucans (derived from dried yeast extract), vitamins C and E, and an oligo-collagen complex. Skin is left feeling buffed and polished.

Elemis Pro-Collagen Marine Cream

ELEMIS PRO-COLLAGEN MARINE CREAM

Where? www.timetospa.com • Selected salons and department stores worldwide

How much? $135

Crème de La Mer may be the most expensive marine-based face cream in the world—the newest addition, "Project Precious," contains the rarest ingredients and costs upwards of $1,500—but the beautifully light Pro-Collagen Marine Cream from Elemis is a much more versatile and affordable option. It is also easier to apply and suits more skin types. Containing the unique *Padina pavonica* algae (a fan-shaped brown algae hand-picked by scuba divers from the temperate waters off Malta), there is also a helping of porphyridum seaweed, chlorella seaweed, mimosa, rose, and gingko biloba. The best way to experience this cream? Have the Elemis Pro-Collagen Japanese Silk Booster Facial, one of the best facials in the world.

Best bargain moisturizers

• **Pond's face cream**. Originally invented in 1846 as a medicine by scientist Theron T. Pond, who discovered it could heal small wounds, this cream became one of the best selling cosmetic creams of the 20th century and many women, young and old, still swear by it.

• **The Body Shop's Vitamin E Moisture Cream** (www.bodyshop.com). The Body Shop's best-selling product is produced solely from plants and includes antioxidants that protect the skin from the elements. At around $14, it's also brilliantly affordable.

• **Olay Complete All Day Moisture Lotion** (www.olay.com). A classic fluid moisturizer, now with SPF15, this absorbs into the skin easily. Great for normal skin types.

• **Nivea Creme** (www.nivea.com). Classic Nivea Creme, in its iconic royal blue and white packaging, is the ultimate multifunctional moisturizer as it can be used on the face, body, and hands. Good for very dry skins.

• **Weleda Skin Food** (health food shops). A skin-saving natural moisturizer, rich in lanolin and essential oils including lavender and sweet orange, which soothe and nourish very dry skin. Can be used on body and face.

Two of the best organic moisturizers

• **Dr Hauschka's Quince Day Cream** (www.drhauschka.com) is a hit with Kate Moss and Sadie Frost. A lightweight, natural cream, it contains quince and beeswax extracts, both of which have protective qualities.

• **Jurlique Recover Gel** is a light, vitamin-rich gel that delivers instant refreshing moisturization in one easy application (www.strawberry.net).

Hairbrush

Mason Pearson

Mason Pearson

Where?

www.tressence.com •

www.beautysak.com •

Better pharmacies

How much?

Large hairbrush with pure bristle, from $65

The Mason Pearson hairbrush is a classic and still the best—a bona fide status symbol for the bathroom. Diana, Princess of Wales, always carried a pocket nylon bristle model in her bag, while top hairdressers the world over— think the kind whose names also grace shampoo bottles— recommend this brand to their clientele. Like many great designs, a Mason Pearson brush is all about the details. Part of the reason the brushes work so well is due to a clever pneumatic rubber cushion, which allows the brush to follow the contours of the head and effectively massage the scalp. Mason Pearson, an engineer from Yorkshire, invented the cushion at the height of the Industrial Revolution while working for the British Steam Brush Works. He also invented the handle, specially designed for comfort and originally made of wood. The original style is still available today, although most are now made from plastic that has been carefully hand-polished to remove any sharpened edges.

Brushes come in four sizes: the "popular large," with six rings of tufts, is suitable for most hair—as a rule of thumb, the longer the hair, the bigger the brush needed. Different hair types require different types of tuft, and Mason Pearson offers three options: natural boar bristle, best for fine to normal hair and less likely to snag the hair than nylon; a mix of nylon and bristle for medium to thick hair and pure nylon—Mason Pearson have developed their own special type of nylon, recommended for very thick hair that tangles. For the folically challenged, there is even a "sensitive" brush with special bristles that further stimulate scalp circulation.

If cared for correctly, a Mason Pearson brush should last a lifetime. If you have spent hundreds on a haircut and highlights, it has got to be worth it!

KENT

Where? www.bathandbody.net • www.baysidebrushco.com • many drugstores

How much? From $12

The Kent NAT20 porcupine and pure bristle brush with wooden handle is a classic. Kent has been making brushes since 1777 and now makes over 250 models—one of which takes over 540 hours to make, a process that includes drying and hand-finishing the satinwood handle. The Kent dressing table comb also comes highly recommended.

FRÉDÉRIC FEKKAI MINI HAIRBRUSH

Where? Frédéric Fekkai salons in Palm Beach FL, Beverly Hills and N.Y.C. • www.sephora.com

How much? About $40

This Hollywood superstar hairdresser's brush is nothing short of perfection: handcrafted in France, made from natural boar bristles and tiny enough, not to say chic enough with its tortoiseshell handle, to carry around in your handbag. Perfect for one-upmanship moments in front of a communal bathroom mirror.

Lip balm

Crème de la Mer

Where?
www.cremedelamer.com • Selected department stores worldwide

How much?
About $45

The most versatile of all beauty products, lip balm eclipses mascara in terms of its desert island must-have appeal. It is usually the first introduction to make-up a girl has, long before the joys of lipstick and eye shadow are ever allowed, and is adored by make-up artists for its ability to add lustre to cheekbones, eyelids, and collarbones. A good lip balm can also smooth scaly elbows, knuckles, and knees. But which is the best? Crème de la Mer may be known for producing the most expensive face cream in the world, but it is the lip balm that really shines. The pale-green balm has a lovely sludgy texture, slight minty smell, and toffee-tinged taste, but it's the instantly soothing effect on chapped lips that makes it the nicest around. Not so much an everyday lip balm—but then not many of us really need lip balm every day—instead use it to indulge when your lips need some intense moisturizing and tender loving care.

Crème de la Mer

SISLEY NUTRITIVE LIP BALM

Where? www.fragrance.com • www.amazon.com • department stores
How much? About $55–$65
A simple pink-and-white tub holds this rich, waxy lip balm that is great for dried out, cracked lips but also as a day-to-day option. Extremely restorative, Nutritive has been designed to take special care of lips that are chapped or dehydrated by extreme weather conditions. The cocktail of natural plant extracts, including hazelnut oil, sunflower oil, shea, and kokum butter, soothe the lips perfectly.

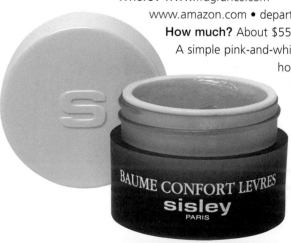

Sisley Nutritive lip balm

KIEHL'S LIP BALM #1

Where? Kiehl's stores worldwide • www.kiehls.com

How much? 1 fl oz jar $8.50

Kiehl's legendary Lip Balm #1, first made in the 19th century, has been a bestseller at Barneys, Bergdorf Goodman, and Fred Segal for decades. It's the quality and sheer simplicity of the product—not to mention that covetable utilitarian packing—that makes it such a hit. The ingredients are all natural—sweet almond oil, vitamin E, aloe vera, wheatgerm oil, and vitamin A.

> *" Just like alcohol or cigarettes, some people seem to be more susceptible to becoming dependent."*
>
> *anonymous, www.kevdo.com*

Kiehl's Lip Balm #1

Cult lip balms

No other beauty product has such addictive appeal—there's even an American website (www.kevdo.com/lipbalm) to help crack the lip balm habit. **Carmex** surely wins the prize for the most addictive brand. Established in 1937, the company is still family owned. The salve contains alum and salicylic acid, which was originally used to treat cold sores, and, according to kevdo, hits you "with a rush that rivals crack cocaine when you first apply it."

Gwyneth Paltrow's favorite is **Smith's Rosebud Salve**—Manhattan's stylish outlet, C.O. Bigelow at 414 Sixth Ave in the Village, sells more than $11,000-worth of this brand every year in mail order alone. The original Rosebud Salve, first prepared in 1892 by a Dr G. F. Smith, boasts a whole host of other uses too—it can be applied to chapped skin, blemishes, nappy rash, and detergent burns. **Perfumeria Gal Madrid** is the most decorative lip balm. With its elegant Art Nouveau style packaging, this Spanish salve comes in 10 different colors and scents and is a bestseller across Europe.

Perfumeria Gal Madrid

Carmex Balm

Mascara

Lancôme Definicils

*Lancôme
Definicils*

Where?
201 Columbus Ave., N.Y.C. •
www.lancome.com • Lancôme
shops worldwide
How much?
$23.50

We all know of at least one woman who refuses to leave the house without coating her lashes in mascara. So what's the big deal? Apparently, our obsession roots back to the most basic, primal of reasons—long lashes signify open eyes, good health, and alertness, still attractive attributes for encouraging the opposite sex. The trick is to find a mascara that does this naturally, without clogging, smudging, flaking or, worse still, irritating the eyelids. After testing as many as we could get our hands on, we've come out with a clear winner: Lancôme Definicils. It's available in black, brown, and a chic navy that goes with everything and looks good on blondes and brunettes, against black or white skin. It lengthens lashes, doesn't smudge, and glides on easily. Undoubtedly one of the star beauty products of our time.

*Yves Saint Laurent
Mascara Volume
Effet Faux Cils*

KANEBO 38°C SILK PERFORMANCE MASCARA
Where? Takashimaya, 693 Fifth Ave., N.Y.C. • 212.350.0100 • www.amazon.com
How much? $21
Outside Japan, this phenomenal mascara is hard to track down, but you can pick it up at Takashimaya in New York and brand new on eBay. It is worth seeking out because those who use it never go back. It glides on and coats each lash with a special silk case that is guaranteed not to smudge in temperatures below 38°C/100°F, hence the name.

YVES SAINT LAURENT MASCARA VOLUME EFFET FAUX CILS
Where? www.yslbeautyus.com • Department stores worldwide
How much? $27.50
Since launching in 2000, YSL's most popular mascara has been a massive hit thanks to its ability to make the lashes appear instantly glamorous—as if you've just applied the most perfect set of false lashes, in fact.

Best for budget lashes
Maybelline's Great Lash mascara is one of the most overrated products in the world—our testers reported smudging and flaking. Instead, for the best budget options, we recommend **Max Factor's 2000 Calorie** mascara and **Rimmel's Extreme Definition Ultimate Lash Separating mascara**, which features a unique metal wand that is more like a comb than the traditional brush and delivers a perfect application of mascara that lasts all day long.

Nail polish

OPI Coney Island Cotton Candy

OPI Coney Island
Cotton Candy

Where?
www.opi.com • J.C. Penney salons • www.shopping.msn.com

How much?
$6–8.50

If there's one item of make-up that instantly makes the wearer appear ultra-groomed, it's nail polish. The polish you choose speaks volumes. Red can transform a look from plain to vixen, black says punk rock, while pearly pink says Barbie-doll cute. But what's the best? Perhaps a natural shade that looks good with pale skin or a tan, works with a casual day look or a high-octane evening do? OPI, the brand favored by Cameron Diaz, Kate Hudson, and Halle Berry, really is the best of the best. With a great consistency, it glides on nicely and stays on for days. There are a massive 250 colors to choose from with cheeky names like "I'm Not Really a Waitress" (a striking red) and "Can't a Berry Have Some Fun?" (a flirty fuchsia pink). The polish you put on is true to the color you see in the bottle, so you know *exactly* what you're getting.

Essie

ESSIE
Where? www.essie.com • Selected salons worldwide
How much? $8

Essie Weingarten, a beauty industry icon, founded this brand in 1981, driven by her desire for the perfect manicure. Available in a mouthwatering array of hues, Essie's nail polishes feature in all the world's leading spas and salons, including Bliss, Canyon Ranch, and La Costa Resort. Popular for their durability and chip resistance, the classic, pretty, neutral shades include Bashful Beige, Pachinko Pale, and Ballet Slippers, all of which feature regularly at haute-couture shows. Madonna, Sharon Stone, and Julia Roberts are fans.

REVLON COLORSTAY ALWAYS ON
Where? drugstores everywhere
How much? $6–11

With colors that are true to the bottle and often outlast more expensive brands, Revlon glides on easily and lasts for up to a week without chipping. Stay Sheer is a good all-round shade.

Revlon
Colorstay
Always On

> **"It is better to apply more thin coats of polish than a few thick coats. The thicker the coat, the longer it takes to dry."**
>
> *Leighton Denny,*
> *celebrity manicurist*

Perfume

Guerlain Shalimar

Where?
68 Avenue des Champs Elysées, Paris •
better perfume counters • www.1stperfume.com •
www.aromaboutique.com

How much?
From $20 for 1.7oz toilet water to $400-plus for 1oz perfume

Guerlain
Shalimar

A good fragrance—a signature scent—is one that instantly sums up a woman's personality. It must be French—a country that views perfumery as the most noble of art forms; and it must be a die-hard classic blend, none of that single-noted nonsense that has been popular for the past few years. A flamboyant history also helps. Shalimar from Guerlain has all of the above.

In the 1920s there was a saying—"there are three things no respectable woman should do: smoke, dance the tango, and wear Shalimar." When it came out in 1925 the scent was described as "racy," "intoxicating," and "impossibly bewitching." Its inspiration? An epic love story from India. Three hundred years before, the emperor Shah Jahan built an amazing garden for his favorite wife, calling it Shalimar or "the temple of love," and filled it with fountains, lakes, marble terraces, rare flowers, and plants. But his wife died and Shah Jahan was left broken-hearted, going on to create the most beautiful mausoleum imaginable for his wife: the Taj Mahal.

In keeping with the scent's exotic inspiration, Guerlain concocted what is generally regarded as the world's first "oriental" scent, a heady mix of bergamot, sandalwood, vetiver, patchouli, and vanilla notes, the latter of which is said to have an aphrodisiac effect—no wonder it caused such a sexy stir when it first came out. Then there's the beautiful bottle with the midnight-blue stop, the pride of any dressing table. The design was originally conceived for the Decorative Arts exhibition in Paris, at a time when colored glass was extremely unusual. The inspiration? Those exotic gardens again, as the shade is said to conjure up images of magical water.

Shalimar isn't sold everywhere, only at Guerlain's dedicated Parisian boutiques and select department stores—Bergdorf Goodman in New York, for instance, where it has been a bestseller for more than two decades. At the Guerlain Institut on the Champs Elysées, Paris, Shalimar obsessives can buy supersized bottles, engraved with their own initials.

BOND NO. 9 CHINATOWN

Bond No. 9
Chinatown

Where? 9 Bond St., N.Y.C. • 212.228.1732 • For other New York branches, see www.bondno9.com • Saks Fifth Ave.

How much? From $125

Launched six years ago, Bond No. 9 is a baby in perfume house terms. More eyebrow-raising still in the rarefied world of haute fragrance, the company is based in New York—and uses the city and its neighbourhoods (from Central Park to Gramercy Park) as its muse. Yet its founder, Parisian Laurice Rahme, has all the right credentials. After working for Creed and Annick Goutal, Rahme branched out on her own, launching a range in star-shaped bottles (complete with a subway token motif, just to hammer home that New York point some more). As gimmicky as all this sounds, Bond No. 9 has been a hit with connoisseurs and customers alike. The range currently contains 26 scents—the newest, Bryant Park, is an homage to the area that hosts New York Fashion Week. Chinatown is one of the label's bestsellers, adored for its unique blend of peach blossom, gardenia, patchouli, tuberose and cardamon. A classic in the making.

FRÉDÉRIC MALLE

Where? 37 Rue de Grenelle, Paris • Barneys N.Y.C. • www.editionsdeparfums.com
How much? From $75

Malle may be new on the scene but he has the right heritage—his grandfather helped develop the fragrance arm of his friend Christian Dior's business—as well as the right attitude, giving some of the world's best noses a free reign to create their own scents. The Paris boutique houses a number of isolation booths, where customers can smell scent in its purest form away from outside pollutants. Already iconic are Lipstick Rose and Cologne Bigarade; Chandler Burr, author of *The Emperor of Scent*, describes the latter as, "the smell of a person in a summer thunderstorm. They are showered and clean, but it is hot, so we can smell their body, neck, clean armpits, and the lovely complex smells of the summer clinging to the skin." Blimey!

Frédéric Malle Lipstick Rose

Five other cult scents

Recently there's been a revival in cult scents, the kind of fragrances that your granny used to wear and that can be instantly identified from 10 feet away. Most are cult for a reason, usually down to an interesting history and heritage. You know these will never be discontinued.

Chanel No. 5

The world's bestselling scent— there's a bottle sold every 30 seconds. It was launched in 1921 and created hysteria when it first went on sale, as it was seen as personifying Coco, the woman every other woman wanted to be. According to legend, the name exists because Coco rejected the first four.

Joy

Launched in 1927, Joy was once "the world's most expensive perfume" (Clive Christian now claims this crown). Rather impressively, it takes over 10,000 jasmine flowers from Grasse in Provence to make a single ounce.

Rochas Femme

Made in 1944 as an exclusive scent for couturier Marcel Rochas' wife, this is a dry "chypre" fragrance with a hint of the masculine. The bottle was inspired by the fullness of Mae West's hips.

Ormonde Jayne Frangipani Absolute

Frequently voted one of the best new scents, and made using only the finest frangipani essence—hence the purer-than-pure result. All of Ormonde Jayne's fragrances are created in-house in her London laboratory. Others include unusual ingredients like pink pepper oil and black hemlock.

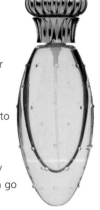

Caron Tabac Blond

Along with Guerlain, Caron is another classy-yet-clever Parisian perfume house. Tabac Blond was created in 1919 and created quite a stir, thanks to its sandalwoody and somewhat masculine scent, a mix of golden tobacco, tuberose, and vanilla. Utterly distinctive—a fragrance some women go batty about.

Red lipstick

Yves Saint Laurent Rouge Pur # 20

Where?
www.ysl.com • Department stores worldwide
How much?
$29

The ancient Egyptians were the first to be seduced by the power of red lips. They used henna to paint theirs, a look that signifies strength. Red lipstick still instills fear in some because they imagine they will end up looking like a freaky clown. Truth is, while not all reds suit everyone—and there are literally thousands of variations from flirty pink reds to siren scarlets—there are some shades—true reds, neither blue-toned, nor yellow tinged—that suit pretty much any complexion. Your lipstick does not need to match your outfit, but it does need to compliment your skintone. A modern classic, this vibrant true red-red from YSL delivers the perfect hit of color, suiting most who try it. The real beauty of this product, apart from the angular packaging emblazoned with the stylish YSL logo, is that it can be worn with ease on a glamorous night out, in the boardroom or to lunch. Don't leave the house without it.

> *"Beauty to me is about being comfortable in your own skin. That, or a kick-ass red lipstick."*
> Gwyneth Paltrow, actress

> *"My all time favorite red lipstick is the one my mother wore. I always begged her for a dab whenever she put it on. I've no idea who it was by, but it came in a heavy gold case and smelled to me of pure glamour. My modern equivalent is Chanel's Rouge Star—I've worn it since the 1980s and I always go back to it whenever I need a fix of red lipstick."*
> Anna-Marie Solowij, Beauty Director, British Vogue

Yves Saint Laurent Rouge Pur #120

*Shu Uemura's
Rouge Unlimited
Red 165*

Nars Red Lizard

SHU UEMURA ROUGE UNLIMITED RED 165

Where? Shu Uemura coutiques in Boston, San Fransisco, Costa Mesa and N.Y.C. (SoHo) • www.shuuemura.com • Department stores worldwide

How much? $23

An intense true red featuring a high-tech pigment which, remarkably, goes on as bright as it looks on the stick. This lipstick also has incredible staying power thanks to its lovely rich texture (yes, it glides on smoothly too). A modern-day classic red; we're sure Marilyn would have approved.

NARS RED LIZARD

Where? www.narscosmetics.com • Sephora, Bergdorf Goodman, Barneys

How much? $24

A wild red with a subtle hint of tangerine makes this a stunning shade for anyone who wears it, but it is particularly drop-dead on blondes. Crucially, it stays on for hours.

Other top reds to suit all skin shades

- **Chanel Fire #65**: A bold, true red.
- **Bésame's Red Hot Red**: A striking, bright red.
- **Guerlain's Kiss Kiss Exces de Rouge 523**: A punchy pinky red that can be worn for day or night.
- **MAC Russian Red**: A sexy, starlet red.
- **MAC Lady Danger**: An arresting, bright red.
- **Laura Mercier Seduction**: A seductive red.
- **Dior's Red Premiere 752**: A lustrous deep pinky red.

Soap

Savon de Marseille

Where?

La Compagnie de Provence, 1 Rue Caisserie, Marseille,
France • www.lcdpmarseille-usa.com • www.amazon.com

How much?

400g bar for $7–$10

Savon de Marseille

We're talking hand soap here, so it needs to look good on your washbasin, not as if you've been squirreling away freebies from hotels. It also needs to smell great—and work! Luckily, Savon de Marseille fits the bill on every count.

Many French women believe Savon de Marseille has magical properties, thanks to the way it is made. Indeed, Marseille has a long tradition of soap making. Its soap is made from oil, alkali from sea plants, seawater—and nothing else. No additives, no artificial colors, no animal fats, nothing. The green bars, which are scent-free, are made with olive oil, the white/beige with palm oil. Each block is stamped with the legend "extra pur 72% d'huile garanti," a standard since 1688.

Marseille's remaining *savonneries* still use the same centuries-old method to make soap. First they brew the ingredients in cauldrons for at least ten days, rinsing repeatedly to remove any excess soda. Each block is then cut by hand—producing a satisfyingly rustic result—and left to dry naturally on racks, a process that can take months. The soap is sold by weight and each block lasts for ages. Incidentally, soap in general is currently enjoying a renaissance simply because it doesn't contain the chemicals found in some shower gels.

AFRICAN BLACK SHEA BUTTER SOAP

Where? www.musefinds.com

How much? $2.95 per bar

There are lots of shea butter imitators out there but Akamuti sells the real deal. Shea butter comes from the nuts of the karite tree, which grows wild in Africa and can't be cultivated. The production process is complicated, laborious and local; Akamuti is a Fairtrade company, so proceeds go towards helping the surrounding community. Black shea butter soap contains no preservatives or additives and aids dry skin, dermatitis, and sunburn. It is also excellent for eczema—many longterm sufferers swear by it.

CLAUS PORTO SABONETE AROMATICO

Where? www.thesoapbar.com • All good Portuguese pharmacies

How much? 12oz bar for $16

The Portuguese and Spanish are fanatical about soap, especially bars that come prettily wrapped and gorgeously scented. Claus Porto's creamy products, handmade in Portugal since 1887, fit the bill perfectly, and include exciting scents like Pear Sandalwood and Red Poppy. Great for gifts.

Home

"Have nothing in your homes that you do not know to be useful or believe to be beautiful."

William Morris, designer, 1834—96

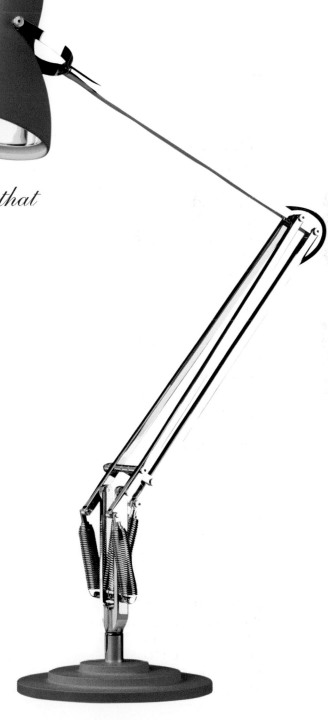

Alarm clock

Jacob Jensen

Where?
www.betterlivingthroughdesign.com
How much?
$40

Jacob Jensen

An alarm clock is the first thing you see every morning, so it had better look good. The Danish designer, Jacob Jensen, excels in making ordinary objects—telephones and doorbells—look extraordinary. He first came to prominence as the chief designer for Bang & Olufsen, the upmarket hi-fi brand, working with them for almost 30 years, and designing more than 80 different products, before branching out on his own. Jensen is now credited with enabling us to view everyday objects with a designer's eye. It is little wonder, then, that he is represented in a number of museums around the world, among them New York's Museum of Modern Art, where he has 19 products in the Design Collection and Design Study Collection.

Jensen's alarm clock was launched in 1999. Like many of his products, the clock is characterized by its sleek lines and subdued metal coloring, and has received the prestigious Red Dot award for industrial design. It looks simple, unobtrusive, and just a little bit *Star Wars*, not to say aesthetically pleasing: the LCD used to display the time has been inversed to make it look more attractive—and less obtrusive for sleepy eyes. The clock is also easy to use—it has just four keys, the concept being that one key equals one function. And for the truly lazy, a similar model is radio-controlled.

Intrepid clock connoisseurs should also head to Japan, land of the all singing, all dancing, voice-responsive mini-robotic alarm clock. The Akihabara area in Tokyo heaves under the weight of the latest in wacky wake-up technology—at surprisingly reasonable prices.

BRAUN TRAVEL ALARM CLOCK
Where? www.goodmans.net • Good electronics stores
How much? $40
This is lo-fi Bananarama-era utilitarian chic at its best for those who don't want digital—and, more importantly, want something that ticks. Fans include Los Angeles-based interior designer Brad Dunning, who puts this matt black clock at the bedside of "almost every client"—think Tom Ford and Sofia Coppola.

LUMIE BODYCLOCK
Where? www.lumie.com • Large British department stores, and branches of Boots pharmacy
How much? From £60/$120
This ingenious new invention regulates the user's melatonin cycle and sleeping pattern by stimulating dawn with a gradually intensifying light. Olympic rowing champion Ed Coode took one to the last games—and just think how early rowers rise.

Bed

DUX 8888

Where?

Duxiana in Vancouver, B.C., and Duxiana stores in 15 states • www.duxbed.com

How much?

$5,950–$11,500

DUX bed

The ultimate modern-day luxury? Getting a good night's sleep, one precious commodity that nowadays money *can* actually buy—albeit at a serious price. Duxiana makes what has to be the ultimate bed, with extra springs that enable the mattress to conform to the sleeper's body shape, great when two people who prefer mattresses of differing firmnesses share a bed. The *outstanding* new DUX 8888 is equipped with boxspring cranks that allow an individual to adjust the mattress height to the level that best supports his or her lumbar vertebrae.

The Swedish company, established in 1926, crafts beds that are passed down from generation to generation, such is their durability. According to independent research, DUX beds are the best for inducing deep sleep, the stage necessary for proper bodily recuperation. A study noted that sleepers on a DUX bed entered the deep sleep phase faster and stayed in the state longer than they did in other beds. If you like mind-expanding rest, if you value your beauty sleep, the DUX 8888 is worth the investment.

SIMON HORN SOLID EUROPEAN WALNUT LIT BATEAU

Where? www.simonhorn.com • Call 336.765.9991 for two dozen U.S. locations

How much? From $4,300 for an adult bed.

Also known as a "sleigh bed," this particular style has won a stack of design awards. Simon Horn is widely credited with kick-starting the renaissance of the French bed. All of his models are built by hand and are said to improve with age. Such is his cachet that Angelina Jolie bought a Simon Horn cherrywood crib for her baby, Zahara.

LOUIS XVI ANTIQUE BED

Where? Top auction houses and antique shops, especially those specializing in French furniture.

How much? You'll end up sleeping in a genuine 18th-century bed only if you've excellent luck and a very deep pocket, but century-old Louis XVI "revivals" can be found for under $2,000.

Beds don't come more rococo than this, with its signature flourishes on the curved head and footboards. Karl Lagerfeld is said to sleep on a particularly ostentatious version embellished with royal blue velvet and gold tassels—the ultimate boudoir furniture.

Bed linen

Pratesi

Where?

829 Madison Ave., N.Y.C. and branches in Beverly Hills, S.F., Boston, Chicago, Houston, Dallas, Palm Beach, Bal Habour • Atkinson's in Vancouver, B.C. • www.pratesi.com

How much?

A basic 480-thread-count sheet starts at about $1,400.

Pratesi bed linen

Enveloping oneself in crisp, white bed linen is undoubtedly the nicest way to sleep. Pratesi is synonymous with expensive bedclothes, considered by many thread-count obsessives (a thread-count is the number of threads in a one-inch square of fabric, and some of Pratesi's are well over 700) as superior to the more ubiquitous Frette. Treated properly, good bed linen is an investment that will last a lifetime—and, since we spend on average a third of our lives in bed, is definitely worth paying for.

Pratesi is an Italian family-run company that has been going for five generations and the manufacturing of each sheet adheres to strict rules. All embroidery is done by hand, for instance, and all apprentices are taught for a minimum of five years before they're allowed to start work on any linen. But it's not just the thread count that, well, counts—of equal importance is the provenance of the cotton, the best coming from Egypt where the yarn actually gets softer and smoother with time and wear. Pratesi are super-picky and use only the top 0.002 per cent.

As sheet snobs will readily attest, getting obsessed with bedding is an expensive habit and, after sleeping on a high thread-count, anything else feels like sandpaper. It's little wonder, then, that according to one Pratesi representative: "Our hardest sell is the first-time customer. Once they buy Pratesi, they're our customers forever."

FRETTE COTTON-SATEEN EGYPTIAN SHEETS

Where? Montenapoleone, 21 Milan, Italy • Frette in Aspen, Beverly Hills, Chicago, Costa Mesa, S.F., N.Y.C. • www.frette.com

How much? From about $1,700 per set (two sheets and two sham cases)

The company was founded by Edmond Frette in the French city of Grenoble in 1860. It soon moved over the border to Italy, where it swiftly established itself as the official supplier to the Italian royal family, as well as the Vatican. Frette's collections offer sheets with interesting borders and crocheted lace insets, and cheaper "hotel" sheets.

D. PORTHAULT

Where? 18 Avenue Montaigne, Paris • 18 E. 69th St., N.Y.C. • 212.688.1660

How much? From $1,100 per set, more for monograms

Truman Capote once said that the difference between the rich and the rest of us was super-fresh vegetables and crisp Porthault sheets. The company was founded in 1925, when Madeline Porthault decided to introduce color and patterns to a world of linen that was previously pure white. The label was a favorite of both Jackie and JFK and the Duke and Duchess of Windsor—both couples slept on monogrammed Porthault sets.

Blanket

Vintage Welsh wool blanket

Where?
Labour and Wait, 18 Cheshire St., London •
www.labourandwait.co.uk

How much?
Prices from $150

Welsh wool blanket from Labour and Wait

OK, so the absolute ultimate may be a Hermès cashmere blanket, which costs a few thousand dollars, but that's simply not realistic.

No, the best blankets actually come from Wales. These are not nearly as soft as cashmere, but what Welsh blankets lack in pleasing tactility, they more than make up for in warmth and durability.

Wales had a thriving weaving industry until the end of the Second World War, when it could no longer compete with the bigger mills of England. The most covetable Welsh blankets, therefore, are the pre-1940s examples. Once found in every Welsh bedroom—the best are double-weave—they are, alas, not quite so easy to track down now, as a number of collectors have got in on the act, not to say certain designers like Ralph Lauren, who has been known to buy up old blankets for inspiration.

To avoid disappointment, head to Labour and Wait, a cultish London hardware store located along a tiny East End street. The couple who own the shop have simple good taste and an eye for detail. The vintage Welsh blankets on sale here will be better than many you'd find in the Welsh Valleys today. Buy one with detachable leather straps—perfect for picnics.

PERUVIAN ALPACA BLANKET

Where? Andean handicraft markets, such as Chinchero and Pisac

How much? $20 to $200 and up

Alpaca, the fleece of llama-like creatures raised in the Andes, is five times warmer than sheep's wool. The best Alpaca buys are found in Peru itself, but shop carefully, as the animal oils on the fibres can leave some blankets smelly. You should also know that blankets sold as alpaca are sometimes mixed with other yarns, including synthetics. An English-language Andean art site (www.andeanart.com) promises 100% alpaca baby blankets at $80; adult sizes cost much more.

PIA WALLEN'S CRUX

Where? www.piawallen.se • www.skandium.com

How much? Approximately $725

Who would have thought something as practical as a blanket could be a design classic? But that's exactly what the Crux blanket is, as many a spread in an interiors magazine will testify. Hand-woven in Sweden, the 100 percent wool blanket comes in three color combos: black and off-white; red and off-white; and potato and off-white.

Candle

Diptyque

Where?
34 Boulevard Saint Germain, Paris • www.beautyhabit.com •
www.bigelowchemists.com

How much?
$55-$60

Diptyque Baies

Once upon a time there was potpourri—and that was it. *And* it didn't smell particularly potent. In the past few years, however, selecting the aroma of one's home has become almost as important as selecting your own signature scent, thanks in part to the trend towards cocooning. Add to that the fact that smell is the most powerful of the senses and you have a mini-revolution on your hands.

Diptyque is king of the candles. Its little glass containers, with their distinctive black-and-white typography, mark out a smart home, while a whiff of their scents is instantly recognizable—unlike many candles, Diptyque's contain a high percentage of natural oils and essences.

The brand has long been popular with the fashion crowd—Karl Lagerfeld burns Cannelle and Héliotrope together. John Galliano, another loyal customer, has even worked with the company to produce his own scent; described as a "warm, deep, and dense fragrance with no flowers at all," it is one of the strongest smelling in the range.

The Diptyque scent that smells the most heavenly is the hot topic of many a beauty site's chatroom. Although popularity is somewhat seasonal—shoppers prefer spicier scents, such as Pomander (cinnamon and orange) and Feu de Bois (firewood) in the run-up to Christmas—the overall bestsellers remain Figuier (fig tree), Tubereuse (tuberose) and, at the absolute top, Baies, a combination of blackcurrant and Bulgarian rose. Such is Baies' cult status that it was the only scent chosen to be converted into a limited-edition black candle to mark Diptyque's 40-year anniversary, and die-hard, won't-burn-any-other-fragrance fans include Natalie Portman, Kylie Minogue, and the supermodel Natalia Vodianova.

For the ultimate Diptyque experience, visit the original wood-panelled Saint Germain store, the address of which is etched on every bottle. Here, experienced sales staff will uncover each jar and encourage you to inhale deeply. Indeed, until as recently as 1999, this is where all the big department stores had to collect their orders from—and Lauren Bacall would actually make an annual Christmas pilgrimage to Paris simply to collect her seasonal scents.

If you still hanker for potpourri, though, the best can be bought from the Florence-based pharmacy Santa Maria Novella, at Via della Scala 16, near the church of the same name.

VOTIVO NO. 96

Where? www.scentsandsprays.com • www.romanzagifts.com • department stores and boutiques around the world
How much? $25
The Red Currant edition, favorite of many a fragrant shopkeeper, has a distinctive berry scent that is pleasingly potent. Treated with care, this candle will burn for 50 hours.

FRAGRANT ORGANIC CANDLES

Where? www.redenvelope.com • www.ecoexpress.com • www.nearseanaturals.com
How much? From a few dollars to $40
Just when you thought a scented candle couldn't be in the least bit harmful, scientists discover that paraffin produces carcinogenic fumes that can be as perilous as passive smoking. If organic candles are not available where you live, hit the web for choices including Botanika and Slowberg at about $35 each. Eco Express offers 15 choices, many for under $10. Lumia has a $7 soy candle.

Chic Candlestick Shopping in Copenhagen

Hygee (hu-gah) is a cuddly concept originating from Denmark, where it is all-pervasive, especially during the country's long, cold winter nights. The word is difficult to translate but essentially points towards a feeling of well-being and conviviality, like taking pleasure from the simple things in life such as a bottle of wine with good company. Suffice to say, the Danes are masters when it comes to atmospheric lighting, and none more so than candlelight: during the winter months. Homes, shops, restaurants and bars rely on candles as a way of masking the harsh outdoor weather, lighting up as early as 9am!

Accordingly, Denmark—or, more specifically, Copenhagen—is the best place in the world to find chic candlesticks.

Your Copenhagen call should be Illums Bolighus at Amagertorv St.; www.royalshopping.com). This multi-floored department store is the ultimate in total design, with everything from duvets to doorstops. Candlestick names to look out for include the glass company littalia (www.iittala.com), which does a fine range of colourful Aalto-inspired votive holders; and Design House Stockholm (www.designhouse.se) for more penny candle holders as well as the striking Nordic Light. Other noteworthy models are Morgens Lassen's Kubus candleholder: first realized in 1960, simple, functional, and cubic in design, it stands the test of time; ditto Peter Karpf's Gemini curvier candlestick (designed in 1965). Both are available from the Danish design company Architect Made (www.architectmade.com).

Finally, those hankering for some old-school classics should head to Bredgade, at the heart of the antiques district. Here you'll find pieces by Bjørn Wiinblad, the highly collectable and much-copied ceramicist, as well as vintage silverware from Georg Jensen.

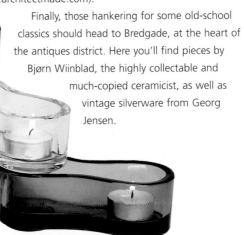

Design House Stockholm candle holders

Chair

Barcelona chair, No. MR90

Where?
Knoll, Inc. 76 Fifth Ave., Floor 11, N.Y.C. • 212.343.4000 • www.knoll.com • www.gabrielross.com

How much?
From $3,900

Because it's the most practical and used piece of furniture, designers have always viewed the chair as an object through which they can make a statement about their design philosophy. In 1929, the German designer, Ludwig Mies van der Rohe, made a chair for the Spanish king, Alfonso XIII, and his queen. It was fashioned in luxurious white leather with a steel frame and looked strikingly contemporary but thoroughly regal too. To this day it remains one of the most desirable chairs of all time, perhaps because it has an almost throne-like quality—it is as opulent as it is modern. Originals, dating back to before the Second World War, fetch more than $15,000 each, and can be identified by their bent, chrome top-rail and feet with a more pronounced curve. Now reissued in a slightly simpler form and structure, with its modern but deeply masculine and luxurious shape, the Barcelona chair remains one of the most desirable pieces of furniture you can buy—the perfect combination of style and function. The Barcelona and other chairs in this spread can be found in many better furniture departments.

Barcelona chair,
No. MR90

LOUNGE CHAIR, BY CHARLES & RAY EAMES, 1956

Where? www.hermanmiller.com (U.S.) • Design Within Reach stores, www.dwr.com • www.gabrielross.com (Canada)

How much? Retails from $2,900 for chair alone.

Charles and Ray Eames fused contemporary aesthetic with ergonomic theory to create furniture that combined the utmost comfort with high-end materials. Created in 1956, the Lounge Chair is a modern interpretation of the traditional club chair, and is now a classic in the history of modern furniture. Finished in rosewood, faced with molded plywood and with sumptuous leather seats, it still reeks of boardroom power and style.

MARCEL BREUER WASSILY CHAIR

Where? www.dwr.com

How much? From $1,600. Miniatures at www.momastore.org for $250

In 1925, the German architect Marcel Breuer began experimenting with tubular steel after being inspired by his trusty Adler bicycle. The outcome was the B3, which became known as the Wassily because Breuer made the prototype for the Russian painter Wassily Kandinsky. Its cubic proportions and the contrast between the fluidity of the steel and tautness of the canvas—Breuer was part of the Bauhaus movement—mean that more than 80 years after its invention, it remains one of the most contemporary chairs on the market.

Jacobsen's 3107 Chair

The ultimate cult chair

With its practical plywood seat, chrome legs, and basic structure, Arne Jacobsen's 3107 chair couldn't be less showy. But like many design classics, that's part of the appeal. This simple, curvy chair was propelled to fame in 1963 when Lewis Morley photographed Christine Keeler, naked and straddling a replica model. You can still buy the chair at House of Copenhagen in Scottsdale, AZ (www.houseofcopenhagen.com) or at Design Within Reach (www.dwr.com) from $370.

Breuer's Wassily Chair

Eames Lounge Chair and Ottoman

Chandelier

Swarovski

Where?
625 Madison Ave., N.Y.C. •
212.308.1710
How much?
Price on request

Unashamedly opulent, a bit of wonderful bling, the chandelier has recently returned to fashion, thanks to fashion-forward designers such as Tord Boontje, Tom Dixon, and Yves Béhar. Chandelier use dates from European medieval assembly halls. Elaborate and decadent examples, with hundreds of candles, lit up the great palaces and villas of 17th-century Italy, 18th-century France, and 19th-century Russia. There's now a new generation of dazzling jewelry for the ceiling.

Daniel Swarovski founded the eponymous brand in 1892 after inventing a device for the precision cutting of crystal gems. Swarovski crystal adorned such celebrity swans as Marlene Dietrich and Marilyn Monroe, whose gown sparkled with 10,000 crystals when she famously sang "Happy Birthday" to President Kennedy. (That dress later sold for a million dollars.) Today, Swarovski crystal chandeliers dangle from the ceilings of New York's Metropolitan Opera House, the Chateau of Versailles, and the Kremlin. The founder's great granddaughter, Nadja Swarovski, has injected excitement into the firm by commissioning some of the world's most renowned designers to create new interpretations of the chandelier, not all of which need a ballroom or boardroom to be shown off.

Swarovski Nest Chandelier by Yves Béhar

LLADRO NIAGARA

Where? 43 W. 57th St., N.Y.C. • 212.838.9771 • www.giftshop.com
How much? $45,000 or $90,000 (larger)
This spectacular, hand-painted chandelier by Bodo Sperlein, for the popular Spanish porcelain company, sparkles with the grace of hundreds of individually suspended fairies, each lit by a fiber-optic cable.

MURANO

Where? Various factory shops on the Venetian island of Murano • www.glasschandeliers.com
How much? From $1,000
This small island, a short water ride from Venice, has been famous for its glassware since 1291, when Italian glassblowers migrated there to escape the hazard of fire easily spreading. Hand-blown chandeliers have been fashionable for over three centuries. Many are elaborate and jewel-toned. Even small ones are pretty.

China

Thomas Goode

Where?
19 South Audley St.,
Mayfair, London •
www.thomasgoode.com

How much?
From £65/$115 for a
bespoke plate

Dating back to 1800 and originally devised by Josiah Spode, fine bone china is a more delicate and prized alternative to porcelain. It is also the ultimate tool for keeping up with the Jones'—show it off by displaying it on dressers, in cabinets, on worktops, and in kitchen cupboards for maximum effect. And if you really want to outdo the couple at number 35, start buying Thomas Goode. The British company was established in 1827 and has a history

Thomas Goode fine bone china

of supplying china to international royalty, that includes over 32 different commissions for the current British royal family alone. To this day, the small, dedicated team of craftsmen take bespoke orders and can incorporate family monograms, logos, type or even a coat of arms onto their bone china plates. Thomas Goode has also recently collaborated with Versace and Paul Smith.

Wedgwood plate & bowl

WEDGWOOD

Where? 158 Regent St., London, • Better department and houseware stores in U.S. and Canada • www.wedgwoodusa.com

How much? Plates from about $17.50 Coined the "Father of English Potters," Josiah Wedgwood founded his own pottery company in 1759 in the village of Etruria that soon became one of the most respected and revered producers of bone china and ceramics in Europe. Wedgwood has recently revamped its image, utilizing the brand's unique and rich heritage, most notably through the

Wedgwood cup and saucer

Robert Dawson collection, which appropriates the classic willow pattern design, enlarging and distorting it so that it looks vibrant and modern. The company has also collaborated with Jasper Conran. The delightful Harlequin line revives old-fashioned patterns and details and, best of all, arrives in delectable packaging with classic designs depicting the signature Wedgwood cameos.

ROYAL DOULTON

Where? www.royaldoulton.com

How much? Cup and saucer from £20/$35

This classic English brand was established in Stoke-on-Trent, Staffordshire, in 1815. Famed for its collectable china figurines, Royal Doulton is also known for its traditional fine china dinnerware and has recently started collaborating with designers including Zandra Rhodes.

The best antique china

In 1710, Meissen of Germany (www.meissen.com) became the world's first porcelain-producing factory. This porcelain can be identified by its blue sword stamp, and was sold mainly from Germany's famous china center, Dresden, where an artistic movement encompassing art, culture, poetry, painting, philosophy—and, most importantly, china—flourished.

Spode, England's oldest pottery company, was one of the first factories to use bone china. Spode is most famous for its classic "Blue Italian" range (www.spode.com), but any of its china is highly covetable, as is that of the chic German brand Rosenthal. Originally established in 1879, Rosenthal continues to produce stylish and elegant bone china (www.int.rosenthal.de).

Left: Rosenthal Pregnant Luise vases

HOW TO SET A TABLE

- A table should always be laid in advance of your guests' arrival.
- You should either lay a tablecloth or, if you want to show off the table, then placemats are a necessity.
- Forks should always be placed on the left of the setting with tines (prongs) facing up, while the knife (with blade facing inwards) should be placed to the right of the setting, along with any spoons that are needed.
- Spoons should only be placed above the plate when you are short on space.
- Side plates should always be placed to the left.
- Napkins should be folded simply and laid on the side plate.
- Glasses should be laid just above the knife and there should be a different wine glass for each type of wine served, plus a separate glass for water.

Cigars

Davidoff Millenium Blend Churchill

Where? Davidoff of Geneva • 535 Madison Ave., N.Y.C. •
212.751.9060 • www.davidoffmadison.com
How much? A box of 10 for $240

Davidoff Special "C" Culebra

For decades, Americans have not been able to import Cuban Cigars—an embargo that started in the fiery hope that Fidel Castro would go up in flames. Instead, many top Cuban tobacco growers were pushed out or fled, taking enough stock with them to seed tobacco farms in the Dominican Republic, where they found soil and growing conditions similar to that of Cuba. Like the top Havanas, Davidoff's Millenium Blend range are hand rolled.

Aficionados consider Davidoff's Millenium Blend range of cigars the best Dominican cigars yet: strong and full of flavor. They're also the most expensive non-vintage cigars on the market—in the cigar world, anything pre 1995 is vintage. The Churchill cigar is the most popular of the Millenium blends. It's of course named after Britain's jaunty World War II P.M., who was rarely seen without a cigar—Winnie's cigar was a Cuban Cohiba.

Davidoff, which started in 1911 in Geneva, was the first merchant to store cigars under perfect temperature and moisture conditions. Davidoff remains fastidious about inventory: each box is coded in a manner that allows, among other things, the tobacco therein to be traced to the field where it was grown.

Age brings out flavor in a cigar. Tobacco quality dictates how many Millenium Blends are produced annually. So holding cigars in optimal storage can prove a wise investment.

Christie's holds twice yearly cigar auctions. Certain vintage Cuban-made cigars are particularly priced. At auction, a box of 25 Chateau Y'Quem, made in "tribute" to the Bordeaux wine estate, went for $8,000.

The Cohiba Robusto Fino is the full name of Churchill's favorite smoke. Today, this cigar is produced in both Cuba and the D.R. They are said to be "nutty, complex, and to smoke perfectly." In New York, Davidoff sells the Dominican Cohibas Robustos—$237.50 for a box of 25.

Another Davidoff offering is the Special "C" Culebra. In Spanish, the culebra is a snake; Davidoff's fat "C" is comprised of three thin cigars (panatelas) twined around each other. These are eight to a box for $242.

Incidentally, some new cigar smokers assume that smaller, thinner cigars are lighter tasting than bigger ones, when actually it's the fatter, well-blended cigars that tend to have the mellower, sweeter flavor.

> **" I like a cigar to really draw."**
>
> **Count Mippipopolous in *The Sun Also Rises* by Ernest Hemingway**

Espresso maker

Gaggia Titanium

Where?

www.gaggia.com • www.wholelattelove.com • Good department and houseware stores worldwide

How much?

$1,300

For the true coffee connoisseur, a good-quality coffee maker is an absolute must. There are hundreds of contraptions, including percolators, vacuum pots, and fully automatic machines that administer this most potent of legal stimulants, but which comes top of the list? We found many that performed well, including Swedish brand Jura and U.S. brand Krups, but we have honed them down to the three mentioned here, which among them include the best fully automated, the most good-looking, and the most iconic.

The first espresso machine was patented in 1901 by an Italian named Luigi Bezzera, but the concept of forcing hot water through a filter of ground coffee beans wasn't developed until the late 1930s. Achilles Gaggia's purpose-built espresso machine, with a piston and lever system, was introduced in 1946 and was widely seen in 1950s coffee bars throughout Europe, so it's no surprise that one of the most superior espresso machines on the market is by this experienced brand. Just press a button and the beans are ground and the coffee measured and brewed into the cup. It looks good too—in sleek stainless steel with a built-in warmer, automatic milk-frother, and electronically programmable portion control.

Gaggia Titanium

ILLY X1 FRANCIS ESPRESSO MACHINE

Where? www.illyusa.com

How much? $900

A favorite with TV and film directors because of its classic good looks, this stylish creation is manufactured by Illy, the first company to create an automatic coffee machine in 1935. With its retro styling, the Illy—designed by Italian architect Luca Trazzi—includes a pump to maintain the ideal pressure for coffee extraction, strong steam pressure for frothing milk, and a brewing handle for ground coffee.

Illy X1 Francis espresso machine

LA PAVONI "PROFESSIONAL"

Where? Via Privata Gorizia 7, 20098, Milan • www.pavonishop.com • Department stores worldwide

How much? $960

It's not automatic and requires a little more patience and expertise to use, but this lovely looking espresso maker from La Pavoni—a company that was founded by Desiderio Pavoni in Milan in 1903 and is credited with inventing the espresso machine—is surely one of the most loveable and classic designs that ever adorned a kitchen.

La Pavoni "professional"

> **" I have measured out my life with coffee spoons."**
> *The Love Song of J. Alfred Prufrock* by T.S. Eliot

KNOW YOUR COFFEE

- **Americano or lungo:** Coffee made from espresso with hot water.
- **Coretto:** An espresso with alcohol in it.
- **Crema:** That velvety thick top layer of coffee.
- **Espresso:** Literally, "of the moment," this is the base of all good coffee. The standard shot for an espresso is 7g (⅓oz) of coffee.
- **Cappucino:** Espresso with frothy milk on the top.
- **Ristretto:** A stronger, even smaller espresso.
- **Tamping:** The process of compressing the ground coffee before the water filters through it.

COFFEE CONFIDENTIAL

- Coffee was discovered in AD 850 by an Ethiopian goat herder who noticed his goats were friskier after eating the berries from coffee bushes.
- The world's first coffee house opened in Constantinople in 1475.
- 57 countries produce coffee in more than 100 growing regions worldwide, including Brazil, Columbia, and Kenya.
- 400 billion cups of coffee are consumed annually worldwide, which means it is the world's second most sought after commodity after oil.

Coffee table

Eileen Gray E1027

Where?
Widely available at better stores
How much?
About $400

Eileen Gray E1027 adjustable side table

While at first glance it seems functional and ordinary, look a little closer and the subtle sophistication of this adjustable occasional table begins to shine through. Check the tinted glass top and smooth curves of the frame—sterile, stark, and functional. The architect and designer, Eileen Gray, developed this timeless and modern occasional table in the 1920s, naming it after her cubist flat-roofed house on the French Cote d'Azur. And while it is not the most expensive, spectacular or decadent of tables, it is in its own quiet way the ultimate design classic, which is why it can be found in the Museum of Modern Art's permanent collection. The joy of the E1027 is that it can fit into practically any context, from a modern warehouse apartment to a small Victorian living room.

> *"Eileen Gray's E1027 table is among the best known examples of early 20th-century furniture design, and like all great examples of design, is both elegant and practical. When she designed the table in the late 1920s, Gray was looking forward to her sister coming to visit and, knowing that she loved breakfast in bed, designed a compact circular table specifically for that purpose."*
>
> **Alice Rawsthorn, Design Commentator**

NAOS PAPILLON

Where? Jensen Lewis, 89 Seventh Ave., N.Y.C. • 212.929.4880 • www.jensenlewis.com
How much? $2,400
This sleek, space-age, double-layered, glass coffee table, which featured in the most recent *Star Wars* movie, has two adjustable surfaces.

Naos Papillon

ANTONIO CITTERIO EILEEN

Where? To find B&B Italia in the U.S., visit www.bebitalia.us • B&B Italia is also in Edmonton, Montreal, Toronto, Vancouver and Winnipeg
How much? From $780
A homage to Eileen Gray's classic E1027 table, this contemporary low coffee table, made for B&B Italia, features sleek steel bases and colored frames.

Cutlery

David Mellor Pride

Where?
4 Sloane Square, London • Hermès in Costa Mesa • Neiman Marcus in Dallas, L.A., Atlanta, McLean and Scottsdale

How much?
42-piece set in silverplate, $650; prices in sterling on request

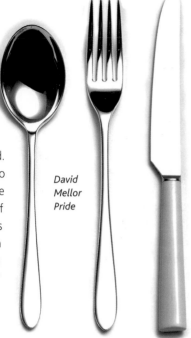

David Mellor Pride

Utilitarian though it is, good quality cutlery, also known as flatware, enhances the look of a dining room and can impress dinner guests no end. The ultimate cutlery should be sleek, streamlined and silver. You want the fork to feel good to the touch, the knife to be a joy to cut with, and the handle of the spoon to fit snugly into the ball of your hand as you scoop up that last piece of apple pie and custard. David Mellor's classic 1950s-style cutlery is a fabulous investment because it has all the right credentials—elegant, sleek, and smooth and an utter pleasure to use. His sets are highly collectable too. Sheffield-born Mellor trained as a silversmith in his teens. Drawing on the historic traditions of Sheffield cutlery, he was inspired to design the Pride line while studying at the Royal College of Art in London. It went into production in 1953, winning one of the earliest Design Centre Awards in 1957. Still manufactured in David Mellor's factory, the Round Building in Derbyshire, it has been in continuous production for over 50 years and is generally acknowledged as one of the most iconic 20th-century modernist designs. Found in stylish homes and museums across the world.

Villeroy & Boch Sereno

PUIFORCAT

Where? 48, Avenue Gabriel, Paris • Barneys, Bergdorf's, Saks in N.Y.C. • Gumps in S.F. • www.porcelaingalleryinc.com

How much? In sterling, silverplate and stainless at corresponding price levels. Founded by Jean Puiforcat in 1820, this elite French silversmith handcrafts cutlery to precise specifications. The silver collection spans centuries of design, from ornate and traditional French patterns to clean-lined contemporary masterpieces. The brand has recently created the elegant three-pronged fork, found in the modern Annecy range.

VILLEROY & BOCH SERENO

Where? Fortunoff, Michael Fina, N.Y.C • better dishware and department stores in North America

How much? About $10 apiece

Perfect streamlined proportions ensure that the Sereno stainless steel set remains desirable. The French brand harks back to 1748 when François Boch established a ceramic tableware business in the French village of Audun-le-Tiche. His business went on to be instrumental in the 1930s' Bauhaus movement.

Desk lamp

Anglepoise Type 3

Where?
The Conran Shop, 407 E. 59. St.,
N.Y.C. • 212.755.9079 •
www.conranusa.com

How much?
From $600

It is maybe not the most spectacular of desk lamps, but the Anglepoise is the most instantly recognizable and iconic, used by scholars, craftsmen, and students the world over.

Automobile engineer, George Carwardine, designed this classic in 1933, using hinges that mimicked the joint of a human arm—and what a clever, novel idea it turned out to be.

The Anglepoise is flexible and balanced and can be held in any position you require. This classic chrome model works almost everywhere you want to be.

TIZIO
Where? www.momastore.org • www.dwr.com
How much? From $280 depending on model
Designed in 1972, Richard Sapper's minimal, energy-efficient aluminium lamp hides the transformer in the base. This reduces voltage, which is conducted through its metal arms to power the lamp, and cleverly eliminates the need for internal wiring. With perfectly counterbalanced arms, this simple but stylish lamp is available in black, white or grey.

AND A FUN ALTERNATIVE—THE SNOOPY LAMP
Where? www.europebynet.com • www.unicahome.com
How much? $840
So named because it resembles a certain canine cartoon character, this lamp is bursting with personality and humor. More than simply something to illuminate the desk, the Snoopy has all the appeal of a little friend.

Anglepoise desk lamp

Fridge

Smeg Refrigerator

Where?
Krup's Kitchen, 11 W. 18th St., N.Y.C.
(212.243.5787) • www.smeg.com
How much?
Approximately $1,750

Smeg Refrigerator

Who would have thought that the retro-referencing Smeg fridge hasn't actually been around since the 1950s, but was instead introduced to the world in 1997? It became an instant design classic, and quite rightly so, its bright colors and curved body making it immediately recognizable.

For domestic divas, labels in the kitchen are as important as they are for other women in the wardrobe. Smeg, therefore, is perfect: free-standing and retro, something that is very "now" in kitchen design, and the absolute antithesis of the 1990s, when everything had to be hidden.

Smeg stands for "Smalterie Metallurgiche Emiliane Guastalla," literally "Metal enamelling factory based in the Reggio Emilia region of Italy," where its factories are still today. The company started in the late 1940s by enamelling metal products for the white goods industry. The idea for the FAB fridge came when the Smeg team noted a general yearning toward more ergonomic shapes in domestic design. They copied the rounded edges of the 1950s' American fridge, adding an enamel exterior in retro shades—such as cream, pastel blue, and pink—creating an immediate hit.

SUB-ZERO

Where? www.subzero.com • The website of the Madison, WI based company displays models, and lists dealers and kitchen designers throughout the U.S. • Western and central Canadians can find subzeros through Bradlee Distributors (www. bradlee.net) • Eastern Canadians should visit www.maroline.com
How much? Prices from $8,425
Another brand that gets kitchen obsessives hot under the collar, this label is the polar opposite of Smeg: think sleek lines and a 100 per cent stainless-steel body. For maximum snob appeal, choose one with a glass front, dedicated wine rack and ice-making facilities.

NORCOOL

Where? www.norcool.com
How much? From $3,500
This is the closest most of us will come to an old-fashioned walk-in larder—a "fridge pantry" with marble shelves. The Norweigen Norcool has accurately, if somewhat snidely, been described as suiting the "middle-class Volvo/Tuscany/farmers-market type who dreams of laying out his unpasteurized cheese and handmade butter on marble." Not available in North America, but a solid choice for your European pied à terre.

Glass / Crystal

Orrefors

Where?
Orrefors factory in Strömbergshytton, Sweden, sells "seconds", but the company store in Orrefors also has discounted, perfect glass • www.orrefors.com • Bloomingdales, Macy's, Fortunoff, Gearys, Michael C. Fine and stores in 11 Canadian cities listed on website

How much?
From $90 for a 9-inch Squeeze vase

The highly respected Swedish glass brand made its name in the 1930s by employing artists to work on its ornamental glass production. Modern designs include the irresistibly tactile "Squeeze" collection, designed by Lena Bergström; the gorgeously chunky, space-age Marin collection by Jan Johansson; and Erika Lagerbielke's voluptuous Venus range, which is inspired by the ripples of waves. An Orrefors vase always makes a statement—even when it is free of flowers.

Orrefors, Squeeze vases

WATERFORD

Where? Visitor's Center, Waterford, Ireland • better tabletop shops and departments • www.waterford.com

How much? $95 for the champagne glass, $500 for the vase (pictured opposite.)

This Anglo-Irish brand was established in 1783, when George and William Penrose founded their business in the port of Waterford in Ireland and started producing high-end glassware. The brand has stylishly stepped into the 21st century by commissioning fashion designers John Rocha, Jasper Conran and, most recently, Marc Jacobs, to design striking and collectable lines. We're in love with Jacobs' engraved champagne bowls and vases.

VENINI & CO

Where? San Marco, 314 Piazzetta Leoncini, Venice, Italy • www.venini.com

How much? From $150

A Milanese lawyer called Pablo Venini established this glassware factory in Murano in 1921, and went on to commission high-profile artists, including Salvador Dali, to design collections in the 1930s. Venini's vintage, brightly colored designs of the 1950s are highly desirable today, with vases fetching up to £5,050 ($10,000) at auction.

Other great glassmakers

Steuben

This Corning, New York, company, founded by Frederick Carder, in 1903, is known for its elegant and beautiful vases and bowls. Each "melted" piece is cut, polished, and engraved by hand.
Flagship: 667 Madison Ave, N.Y.C.
www.steuben.com

Jeanette Hayhurst Fine Glass

A glass gallery specializing in fine specimens from the 17th to the 20th centuries.
32a Kensington Church St, London W8

Iittala, Finland

This Finnish company sells contemporary glassware—functional but highly stylized.
www.iittala.com

Locchi

A Florentine company that specializes in beautiful cut-glass decanters and glasses.
www.locchi.com

Lalique

Master goldsmith, René Lalique, led the Art Nouveau jewelry movement in the 1890s and later became a top glassmaker; creations include the now iconic bulbous glass rings.
www.lalique.com

Pasabahçe Beykoz

Turkey's handmade glassware industry is now among the world's most innovative. Come here for marvellous Ottoman-inspired glass tableware.
Tesvikiye Caddesi, 177, Istanbul

Minna Rosenblatt Gallery

The world expert on the stained glass lamp shades of Louis Comfort Tiffany.
961 Madison Ave, N.Y.C.
212.288.0250

Waterford's Elizabeth Champagne Saucer by Marc Jacobs

Waterford's Robert Vase by Marc Jacobs

Juicer

Champion 2000+

Where?
www.championjuicer.com • www.costplusjuicers.com
How much?
Approximately $175 for home model

This is a juicer with a cult following thanks to its hippie roots. Champion juicers have been going since 1955, and are still made by the same family firm, based in California, a juice-friendly state if ever there was one. The 2000+ weighs a ton, takes up too much space in the kitchen and is far from pretty, but that's not the point—it has been scientifically proven that juice from the Champion retains more nutrients from the original fruit or vegetables than any other model on the market. Which, quite frankly, is any juice-a-holic's dream. This nutrient-containing ability is due to the masticating action of the cutter—a rotating stainless-steel blade that can reach nutrients, even those locked away in the skin.

Champion
2000+ Juicer

The Champion is especially skilled with hard fruit and vegetables, is a doddle to clean, and easy to use—you simply feed through the fruit or vegetable, and the pulp comes out of the other end looking rather like a "sausage." Despite the scores of new juicers on the market today, this is the model still cited as the best by many raw food experts.

MAGIMIX LE DUO
Where? www.chefscatalog.com
How much? $300
With a centrifugal system, meaning the juicer spins the juice from the pulp, this is quiet to use—a blessing in the morning if others in the house are still sleeping—looks good and comes in a range of colors. With juice bars springing up all over the shop—charging upwards of $4.50 a pop—the reasonably priced Le Duo makes financial sense. It even comes with a recipe book.

WARING JUICE EXTRACTOR
Where? Selected health and health-food stores • www.amazon.com
How much? From $75–$175
Another American brand that has been going since the 1960s, this one is easy to operate. It is also good with hard fruit and vegetables.

Knives

Global

Where?
Various cookware specialists and department stores • www.chefknivestogo.com

How much?
From $389 for a six-knife set

Very sharp, very chic, and very expensive, Global knives are made in Japan—a country with a history of producing sharp products, think of the samurai and their swords—and are on every kitchen snob's wish list.

The reason they're so sharp is because the blade is sharpened to a point, instead of bevelled like other knives. Another idiosyncrasy lies in the handle: received wisdom decrees that a good knife should have a "full tang"—in other words, a blade that goes through to the handle in one piece. Global knives, however, consist of three pieces—the blade and two dimpled metal pieces that make up the handle; all welded together to create a knife that's surprisingly light. A carefully measured amount of sand inside the hollow handle provides perfect balance for the user.

Given Global's worldwide prestige, the company is relatively young—started by Komin Yamada in 1985. All knives are still made in Japan. The six-knife block is everything the amateur cook could ask for, and looks less industrial than the usual Global magnetic block.

With regular sharpening and due care—wash and dry immediately after use, and never in a dishwasher—a Global knife will last a lifetime.

Global Knives

HENCKELS
Where? Good kitchenware stores • www.chefknivestogo.com
How much? From $25 and up per knife.
Global's closest competitors are both German companies: Wusthof-Trident and Henckels. The latter is better known and has been making knives since 1731.

LAGUIOLE
Where? Better kitchenware stores • www.laguiole.com
How much? Set of six steak knives about $700, depending on style and purchase place.
These knives, first made in 1829 in the French province of the same name, were initially used by shepherds. Today Laguiole make the best steak knives. Especially attractive is the box of six, with each handle crafted from a different type of wood, something that would make any table setting instantly eye-catching.

Stove

Aga

Where?
250 dealers in the U.S. and
Canada • www.aga-ranges.com
How much?
$8,000–$12,000

Aga Oven

Ovens can make people ridiculously territorial—the chef Gordon Ramsay, for instance, once threatened to lock his domestic model away from his wife. A great range can also sell a house, especially if it's an Aga.

Agas are special. They use radiant heat so the oven is always ready; the result is that the food is moister than usual, with the flavor sealed in. An Aga's temperatures aren't readily adjustable, as they are on conventional ovens; instead, cooks must rely on intuition, yet once the Aga owner understands his or her stove's subtleties, anything is possible. Or so the theory goes. Dedicated recipe books for Aga users instruct on where certain foods can be cooked and for how long. A poppadom can be ready in seconds, for instance, by trapping it under the lid of the boiling plate.

The Aga was actually invented in Sweden in 1922 by Dr. Gustav Dalen. The aim of the Nobel Prize-winning Dr. Dalen was to create a modern stove for his wife.

A four-oven Aga is the most covetable—this means you can do baking and roasting separately, as well as keeping plates hot in the "warming oven"—and is available in a range of jolly colors; Aga snobs prefer cream. Ovens come with a wire-folding toaster that can toast four slices at a time when placed on the hotplate—obsessives insist that this makes the perfect slice of toast. Agas can also be used for ironing, to open jam jars, and dry out boots … no wonder such cooks as Billy Joel and Sarah Jessica Parker go ga-ga for Agas.

VIKING RANGE

Where? Many kitchen appliance stores • www.vikingrange.com
How much? $3,700–$11,000
The Viking doesn't have a restaurant pedigree—which is a good thing. This is a professional quality stove designed for home cooks with the same snob-factor appeal for Americans that the Aga has for Brits. Like an Aga, a Viking range can be bought with dual ovens and comes in a range of finishes, including forest green and cobalt blue. Expect kitchen envy with one of these.

LACANCHE CLUNY STEEL RANGE

Where? www.lacancheusa.com
How much? From $7,000
"The couture gown of ovens," according to *Vogue* magazine, the Lacanche Cluny is seriously smart, with five burners of various sizes, two ovens, and storage drawers. Found in stylish urban kitchens.

Paint

Farrow & Ball New White

Where?
www.farrow-ball.com

How much?
$60-$70 per gallon

Farrow & Ball New White

This is the new magnolia: a creamy white that is warmer than most and ideal either on its own or to complement other colors. If glossy brilliant white looks too bright, then New White is more mellow, never looking too modern nor too stark.

Part of New White's appeal is down to its pigment that includes raw umber (a natural brown clay), yellow ochre and a touch of burnt umber to give the shade warmth. The end product has a soft, almost powdery finish, something that is a trademark of posh paint-makers Farrow & Ball.

Yet another trademark is the company's crazy color names: Eating Room Red (a deep, aristocratic shade), for instance, or Elephant's Breath (a soft grey). Yet it is their palette of whites for which the company is most renowned—All White, Old White, Strong White and White Tie to name but a few—and choosing exactly which one to use has driven many an amateur decorator mad. New White is the brand's bestseller, created when Off White (another popular shade and the whitest white the British National Trust dared to use on the restoration of its properties), looked too grey.

Farrow & Ball was founded in 1947, but the company really came to prominence when two old school friends, Martin Ephson and Tom Helme, bought the company in 1992. The duo revamped the brand while staying true to its roots, and still manufacture all the paint they sell using traditional methods. They also use lots of pigment—up to 30 per cent more than other manufacturers—resulting in a greater depth and luminance of color.

Farrow & Ball is a byword for smart interior taste, the brand chosen to paint the whole of Highgrove, the Prince of Wales's estate. The company has a "to-the-trade" showroom in New York as well as the showrooms listed on the left. Its website lists several additional stores that carry F&B paints, including one in Greenwich, CT, and several more outlets in Canada.

Farrow & Ball Showrooms

Washington Design Center
300 D St. SW
Suite 622
Washington DC
T: 202.479.6780
e: washington@farrow-ball.com

One Design Center Place
Suite 337A
Boston, MA
T: 617.345.5344

8475 Melrose Ave
West Hollywood
Los Angeles, CA
T: 323.655.4499

Farrow & Ball Canada Inc.
1054 Yonge St.
Toronto, Ontario
T: 416.920.0200
e: farrowball@bellnet.ca

Piano

Yamaha baby grand

Where?
www.yamaha.com
How much?
Approximately $12,000–$16,500

"No home is complete without a piano." So said Elton John to David Beckham when giving advice on which piano he should buy as a present for his wife. Posh received a black Yamaha baby grand—Elton's favorite; he also plays on a Yamaha concert grand—with "For My Darling Victoria" written in gold leaf under the lid.

A Yamaha baby grand is half the size of a concert grand piano. It fits into a smaller space than most baby grands, as it has been designed for the modern house—only a mansion could comfortably cope with a full-sized grand piano. Yet the smaller size doesn't mean a compromise on sound. Grand pianos in general produce a better, more full-bodied sound because their strings are longer. An open lid on a grand improves the sound further letting it flood the room.

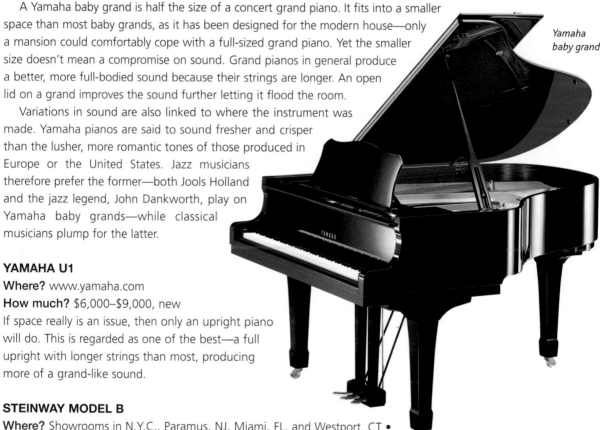

Yamaha baby grand

Variations in sound are also linked to where the instrument was made. Yamaha pianos are said to sound fresher and crisper than the lusher, more romantic tones of those produced in Europe or the United States. Jazz musicians therefore prefer the former—both Jools Holland and the jazz legend, John Dankworth, play on Yamaha baby grands—while classical musicians plump for the latter.

YAMAHA U1

Where? www.yamaha.com
How much? $6,000–$9,000, new
If space really is an issue, then only an upright piano will do. This is regarded as one of the best—a full upright with longer strings than most, producing more of a grand-like sound.

STEINWAY MODEL B

Where? Showrooms in N.Y.C., Paramus, NJ, Miami, FL, and Westport, CT • www.steinway.com • www.beethovenpiano.com
How much? Depending on age, material, and condition, anything upwards of $32,000
For the snob-factor, Steinway & Sons is the ultimate brand, not to say the most expensive. Found in concert halls across the world, along with Bosendorfers and Bechsteins, Steinways are crafted using the finest materials and consist of 12,000 parts that are all made by hand—owners believe this gives each Steinway a unique soul. They are even an investment, worth more the older they become. The seven-foot Model B is most popular.

Quilt

Traditional Amish quilt

Where?
The Old Country Store, 3510 Old Philadelphia Pike,
Intercourse, PA 17534 • www.theoldcountrystore.com

How much?
As shown, $685 for Queen-size

Traditional Amish quilt

The best place to find some *Little House on the Prairie*-style chic is Lancaster County in Pennsylvania, home to America's oldest Amish community and arguably the best quilters in the world.

Quilts are now the third-biggest source of income for most Amish communities, and the quilts of Lancaster County are regarded as having the finest needlework and most unusual color combinations, often set against a darker background.

Look closely, though, and you can see that the stitching isn't always super-smooth—according to lore, Amish quilt-makers deliberately mis-stitch now and then, as they believe only God can be perfect.

For the widest variety of quilts, head to The Old Country Store, housed in a Victorian-era general shop. Here you'll find hundreds of quilts, all locally made using skills that have been passed on from mother to daughter. The best quilts come from a single quilter—one pair of hands means a uniformity of stitching—and some can take up to 800 hours to make, hence the high prices. A percentage of each sale goes to the quilter.

Vintage quilts are the most covetable. In the 1960s there was a quilt revival—something that has continued to this day. The revival was prompted by a wish to raise Appalachian income and pride by encouraging marketing cooperatives dedicated to selling the finest of traditional crafts. As more Americans became interested in homespun treasures, interest in the beuatiful quilts of the Amish also soared.

Be aware that caring for an antique quilt is challenging and that restoring one may be impossible. Old quilts can stand niether dry cleaning nor vigorous washing. Attack a stain or discoloring gently with a moist cotton swab dipped in a cool, soapy water, but be aware that discoloring may be permanent. Fragile fabrics may fray at the first attempt at scrubbing, and colored pieces may run if they become wet.

Nowadays, many quilts have moved from the bed to the wall, becoming bona fide museum pieces in the process, and are sometimes worth several hundred thousand dollars.

HALF-KILO INDIAN QUILT

Where? Maharani Art, Tambako Market, Jodhpur, India

How much? From approx $70

Some of the best heavy Indian quilts come from Jodhpur and one reputable outlet is Maharani Art, a fabric store in the tangled back streets of the old city. Prices are notably higher than your average Indian market stall, but the quality is higher too—fashion houses such as Hermès, Stella McCartney, and Etro buy fabric from the same distributor, and you can rest in the knowledge that, because it's a cooperative, the quilters are getting a decent wage.

Rug

The Rug Company

Where?

88 Wooster St., N.Y.C. • 8202 Melrose Ave., LA • 124 Holland Park Ave., London W11 •
www.therugcompany.info

How much?

From $2,000

This Paul Smith design for The Rug Company featured in the Sex and the City *movie*

A good rug is hard to find—something The Rug Company knows all too well. In 1997, when the business was initially launched by groovy husband and wife team Christopher and Suzanne Sharp, rugs were in something of a style rut: fusty, dusty, and utterly unchic. The Sharps introduced playful prints, brought big-name designers on board, and created iconic rugs in the process: say Paul Smith's multi-colored swirly number, Vivienne Westwood's tea-stained Union Jack, and Marni's rangy flowers. Each of the rugs is lovingly and painstakingly hand-knotted in the traditional way using hand-spun wool. The company also does limited-editions with designers like Ron Arad, who created a memorable rug that spelt out the word "S-H-A-G." The Rug Company's major role in the revival of rugs has made the Sharps design heroes: their pieces make a fantastic focal point to any room, not to say an "investment" item. When you move home, you can role up your Rug Company rug and take it with you. You can't do that with a fitted carpet.

KASHGAI AKA QASHQAI WEAVERS

Where? The market in Isfahan, Iran • ABC Carpet & Home, Manhattan, Bronx, Hakkensack, NI, Delroy Beach, FL • Liberty, Harrods, London • www.oldcarpet.com • www.spongobongo.com

How much? From $500–$600 per square meter (yard)

Rugs from Persia—modern-day Iran—are still considered the best in the world. Many fine rugs come from the ancient city of Isfahan, once a stop-off point for caravans travelling along the Silk Road, where thousands of rugs can still be found in dusty piles at the market. Some of the best come from the Kashgai, a nomadic tribe based in southern Iran. Their rugs are hand-knotted using only the wool from the shoulders and neck of the sheep; the result is a rug that is both fine and firm. The rugs are spun by the women of the tribe and no children are involved in production, an unusual guarantee in the carpet trade. One of the reasons Iranian rugs are so good is that they are used by the same people who weave them—and they desire a quality product just as much as you do. Many sold have been used by the tribe for up to 40 years, but will still be in tip-top condition, since they will only have been walked upon in stockinged feet. However, it is always worth checking that any wear is even and that the fringing is in a good condition.

TURKISH RUGS

Where? A.B.C. Carpet and Home, 881 Broadway, N.Y.C. • 212.376.7574 • www.abchome.com
How Much? From $799
Turkish rugs are less expensive than Persian, yet a tasteful modern example is still hard to find.

Stepevi Turkish rug

" I go to Morocco two or three times a year for inspiration. One of the best buys is rugs and carpets. I have a hoard of cream sequinned carpets—originally used as wedding blankets—that cost about £40, and I've seen them in Liberty for £250. I also invested in a proper carpet last year, a 1960s Beni Ourane. All are unique with distinctive black and white designs—in fact, World of Interiors did a piece on them recently—and although not cheap they're a lot less than buying them elsewhere."

Olivia Morris, shoe designer

HOW TO HAGGLE

For many in Africa and Asia, bartering is a national sport. And, like any sport, there is a stringent set of rules. First, patience is crucial. The correct bartering etiquette requires time—something most merchants have in spades—as it is considered respectful to think carefully when parting with something as important as money.

Once you show even the slightest iota of interest, the game begins. Ask the price, and in a merchant's eyes you've already bought it. Sellers will start at double, triple, even ten times the amount they'd expect you to pay. Your first response should be a method-actor-worthy look of horror that is followed by a bid somewhere below half the asking price. Mentally decide on the top price you'll pay and stick with it. Once you reach it, keep repeating it over and over—the merchant will eventually get the point. And once you've both decided on a price, it is extremely rude to back out.

When dealing with antiques, ask the price first before enquiring about its provenance—that way, you'll sound like a seasoned buyer. You can also use articles you've brought from home—pens, T-shirts, etc.—as part of the deal, especially if the seller has expressed an interest.

It is also worth knowing that most merchants have their own pecking order of perceived wealth. The Japanese are charged the highest prices, then the Americans, followed by Europeans. If you're after a genuine bargain, pretend you're from some obscure country. And don't feel bad—merchants are canny and would never part with anything without turning a profit.

Sofa

Jasper Morrison Cappelini Elan

Where? The Conran Shop, 407 E. 59 St., N.Y.C. • 212.755.9079 • Current, 629 Western Ave., Seattle • 206.622.2433 • www.unicahome.com

How much? From $5000

If a chair is the most functional item of furniture in the house, then a couch is the most leisurely. An object designed for relaxing, reclining and lounging, it is the piece of furniture that signifies time off. So which is the best style? There are thousands of different designs to choose from, from the traditional Chesterfields to the minimal Scandinavian models, but none with quite the same style and grace as the Jasper Morrison Cappelini Elan. Minimal and angular, the beautifully simple Elan sofa epitomizes Morrison's quiet, timeless aesthetic, and would look as good in a brownstone as it would in a modern loft apartment.

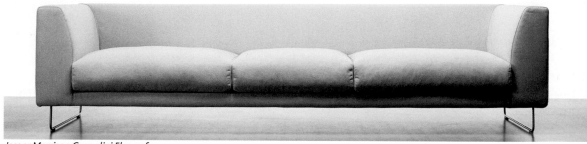

Jasper Morrison Cappelini Elan sofa

ANTONIO CITTERIO CHARLES

Where? B&B Italia, 150 E. 58th St., N.Y.C. • 138 Greene St., N.Y.C. • 290 Townsend St., S.F. • 8801 Beverly Blvd, LA • 752 Harvard Ave. E., Seattle • www.europebynet.com • for other locations: www.bebitalia.com

How much? From $12,000

The ultimate modular sofa—rectangular, free cushions are placed against a low backrest that make it appear chic and modern. It is also possible to arrange peninsula-shaped compositions in the center of the room.

Antonio Citterio Charles sofa

STUDIO 65, BOCCA MARILYN LIPS SOFA

Where? www.modani.com • www.nova68.com
How much? $1,000

You can't get a more inviting couch than one in the shape of a luscious pair of red lips. Inspired by Salvador Dali's Mae West sofa, made in 1936.

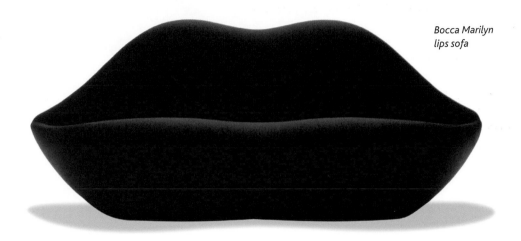

*Bocca Marilyn
lips sofa*

Other sofa suppliers

Donghia

Angelo Donghia's furniture company displays American design at its very best. Here you'll find exuberant, impeccably made sofas that fuse classic shapes and modern styling details, for example the beautiful Borsalino collection, which was inspired by the Caribbean style of the 1930s and 1940s.

Donghia Furniture, Mount Vernon, NY, 914.662.2377
www.donghia.com

Mascheroni

This luxury Italian brand specializes in large, sleek leather sofas, which fuse traditional manufacturing methods with cool contemporary design. The ethos behind this brand is passion, quality and craftsmanship.
www.mascheroni.it

Three iconic sofas

Florence Knoll, Model No. 1205

This clean-lined and elegant sofa was designed in 1954 as part of Florence Knoll's quest to create the ideal "fill-in pieces." The solid-wood frame and square tubular steel with a polished chrome finish give it superior stability and style. www.allmodern.com and www.retromodern.com, from $7,800

George Nelson's Marshmallow sofa, 1956

This classic has a painted tubular steel frame with vinyl-covered latex foam-filled cushions. Currently available at www.hermanmiller.com, from $2,700

Marcel Breuer F-40 cantilever couch, 1930–1931

Chromed tubular and flat steel frame with a leather upholstered seat and back cushions, this design classic has been reissued by Tecta.

Stationery

Smythson

Where?
4 W. 57th St., N.Y.C. • 212.265.
4573 • www.smythson.com

How much?
Bespoke from $375 for 100 cards
and envelopes

Smythson
stationery

Stationery is having a bit of a moment. Maybe it's a reaction to the prevalence of emails, maybe a yearning back to school days when there was always a competition to have the best paper and pens in class. Whatever the reason, when it comes to stationery tread carefully, as the style you choose is very much a statement of how you wish the world to see you. It's all about image, about getting the right size, weight, color and engraving font. There are stationery snobs out there who will actually turn over letters to check the watermark. So beware.

Smythson stationery will earn you kudos. They are Queen Elizabeth's favorite stationers with the maximum four royal warrants and have been used in the past by everyone from Sigmund Freud to Grace Kelly. Modern clients include Gwyneth Paltrow, who, as well as using the bespoke service, bought 20 boxes of apple-motif cards when her daughter, Apple, was born. Madonna and her daughter, Lourdes, also have their own individualized sets—the pop icon is very hot on her offspring sending "thank you" notes, apparently.

The company was founded in 1887 when Frank Smythson started producing lightweight diaries—Princes Harry and William won't use anything else. Stationery quickly followed, as did a bespoke service, which nowadays includes hand-engraved motifs (there are over 100 to choose from, ranging from a ladybird to a black stiletto); tissue-lined envelopes in a variety of colors, hand-painted borders, and different typestyles. The lettering is all hand-engraved, which means the lines are just so and the ink is of a perfect intensity.

And the color? Favorites include Park Avenue Pink, Bond Street Blue, and, of course, Nile Blue, the brand's signature shade, found on all its packaging and inspired by a trip Frank once took to Egypt.

CRANE & CO.

Where? www.crane.com • 59 W. 49th St. (Rockefeller Center) N.Y.C., and fine stationers throughout U.S. and Canada

How much? Monogrammed 50-note sets from $200

Crane & Co. is where the White House gets its stationery and is also the supplier of paper for the U.S. dollar bill.

R. NICHOLS

Where? www.r-nichols.com

How much? New York series of eight notecards, $15

Distinctive, fashion-led designs—a typical motif is a woman rushing for a New York taxi laden down with shopping bags. R. Nichols is Manhattan based, perfect for Carrie Bradshaw acolytes everywhere.

Table linen

Busatti Melograno

Where?

14 Via Mazzini, Anghiari, Toscana, Italy • Visit www.busatti.com for Busatti shops in Montreal and 12 surprising U.S. cities

How much?

Tea towel imports from $15

Busatti Melograno

Every host or hostess needs to know how to dress a table beautifully. And like most things, good table dressing starts with a good foundation.

Some of the most beautiful table linens can be found at Busatti. The store is an experience in itself; situated inside the pretty Tuscan walled town of Anghiari, Busatti's showrooms are housed in a vaulted 16th-century building. The family-run company was founded in 1842 and still uses the same 19th-century techniques and antique looms. All the dyes are vegetable-based and the hems are stitched by hand. The result is of a much higher quality than most of us are used to today—the fabric is soft yet washable, *very* necessary for table linen, and indeed these tablecloths are investment pieces that will last a lifetime.

Busatti's clientele include Miuccia Prada and Valentino, both fans of the company's custom-made service. Off-the-peg designs have an aristocratic feel—think plenty of jacquards in rich hues—perfect if you hanker after the stately home effect. The Melograno range (pictured above) feels more modern. Its fresh stripes are available in a number of colors and the fabric is a mix of linen and cotton. Busatti also makes bed linens, which are again wonderfully soft, and upholstery materials.

GIVERNY

Where? www.pointshop.com

How much? Tablecloths from $60

This classic red-and-white checked pattern is perfect for anyone aiming for the shabby-chic bistro effect. Just add tumblers full of red wine and a dripping candle.

DESIGNER'S GUILD

Where? 267 and 277 Kings Rd., London • www.designersguild.com

How much? From $14 for a set of 4 placemats

Add a splash of color to a table of white porcelain plates with a bold print from Designer's Guild. Their signature florals in citrus shades should perk up even the dullest of dinner parties.

Teapot

Mariage Frères

Where?
30 Rue du Bourg-
Tibourg, Paris •
www.mariagefreres.com

How much?
$145/€120

Loukoum teapots

The French are in the throes of a love affair with tea, hanging out in tea salons and treating different blends with the kind of reverence they would normally reserve for fine wine or good coffee.

So it makes sense that Paris has also become the premiere teapot-purchasing destination in the world. Mariage Frères is the city's most celebrated salon—Hugh Grant is one of many celebrity fans of this curiously olde-worlde establishment in the heart of the Marais district, and the actress Isabelle Adjani takes tea here every week.

There is a museum on the second floor, up a very creaky staircase, but the main pull is the shop itself—a veritable tea heaven, crammed with hundreds of varieties of world-class blends, including more than 50 types of Darjeeling. The teas are displayed in row upon row of canisters, ready to be dispensed into pretty little tins, the pride of any kitchen.

Also displayed in the shop's wooden cabinets are teapots, some cast iron, some porcelain, but all extremely stylish. Their Loukoum design is one of the best, a pleasing combination of Oriental wit with Western overtones in a range of striking colors: think turquoise, orange, and coral. A matching Japanese-style handle-free cup is also available.

Mariage was one of the first merchants to introduce tea to France in the 17th century, yet its teas have only been on sale to the general public since the 1980s; before that, only a select few, including Russia's last tsar, Nicholas II, were deemed sufficiently worthy of sipping the brews. Nowadays, Mariage Frères is open to all and, since tea parties are the new cocktail parties, there's no excuse to lay a less-than-chic table.

TAKASHIMAYA

Where? 693 Fifth Ave., between 54th and 55th Streets, N.Y.C.• 212.350.0100 •
www.ny-takashimaya.com

How much? From $45

The Manhattan outpost of this Japanese department store sells only the most design-conscious oriental objects. Takashimaya's weighty cast-iron teapots are part of the traditional—and very ritualized—way the Japanese take tea. To get an idea of the experience, visit the Tea Box, Takashimaya's in-store café where the sushi is cut to look like finger sandwiches. *Kawaiiiii!* (cute!), as the Japanese might say.

ROYAL ALBERT OLD COUNTRY ROSES

Where? www.royaldoulton.com • www.amazon.com

How much? From $92 for a large teapot

You can't talk teapots without mentioning this one, officially the world's best-selling design. A chintz-tastic pattern—and, quite frankly, as English as it gets.

Tiles

Hand-painted Portuguese azulejos

Where?
Sant'Anna Showroom, 95 Rua do Alecrim, Lisbon • Factory, 98 Calcada da Boa Hora, Lisbon • www.fabrica-santanna.com • www.freersacklershop.com

How much?
$36 for a 4-tile pattern

Portuguese tiles

Whiz around the streets of Lisbon and you'll quickly realize that tiles *(azulejos)* are omnipresent, decorating the exteriors of the most innocuous of buildings and the interiors of everything from barbershops to butchers.

Sant'Anna is regarded as one of the best tile producers in the world. The company specializes in historic reproduction tiles, but will also make custom pieces. This traditional producer hasn't changed much in the last 200 years and all tiles are still made by hand; the pattern stencilled onto a plain white tile before being painted and then glazed. Helpful showroom staff will make your choice less time-consuming, pulling out heavy panels of completed sets so customers can see the design in its full glory. As well as reproductions, there is a small selection of antique tiles, mostly framed for use as stand-alone decorative pieces. Sant'Anna will ship your tiles home so there's no need to worry about them weighing down your luggage.

HAND PAINTED MORROCAN TILES
Where? www.Berbertrading.com
How much? From $4.50 per tile
Morocco is another country famed for its tiles, and those from Fez are superior to any found in Marrakech, as Fez clay is rich in manganese and therefore more scratch-proof. Try the workshops in the Quartier de Poterie, or the Société Fakhkhari. Situated just outside the medina, this is a pile-it-high store with the advantage, for anyone suffering from haggle-fatigue, of fixed prices—although this being Morocco, deals can still be made, especially if you pay in cash. Since the factory is next door to the shop, prices are rock bottom and for once the quality is superb. The Societé also produces whole mosaic floors that can be shipped anywhere in the world.

TALAVERA SANTA CATARINA
Where? Santa Catarina Workshop, Cholula, Puebla, 77820, Mexico
How much? From around $10 for a mural tile
Like Lisbon, Puebla in Mexico is a city covered in tiles. Tin-glazed "Poblano Talavera" tiles are a speciality, although there are only a few authentic workshops remaining. Talavera Santa Catarina is one of them—here you'll find the real deal in bright cobalt blues, yellows, greens and ochre.

Toaster

Dualit

Where?

Various cookware specialists and department stores • www.williams-sonoma.com • www.amazon.com

How much?

$240 for a 2-slot, $315 for a 4-slot model

A kitchen classic that's spawned scores of imitators, and justly so, as the Dualit toaster does all the right things—it looks good *and* makes great toast.

The British company Dualit has been making toasters for more than 50 years and its models are a favorite with all the top hotels, where a constant supply of hot toast is a must for the daily routine of breakfast. Instead of popping up, the Dualit is manually operated, switching itself off when the toast is ready and keeping it warm until you're set to add butter. The bread slots are wider than most, so they can accommodate waffles and teacakes; add a sandwich cage, and Dualit can also do a cracking toastie. Each toaster is assembled by hand and you can choose from two-, three-, four- or six-slice options in a number of fashionable retro colors, including lavender, duck-egg blue, and fire-engine red, as well as chrome.

Dualit Vario Combi 2+1 toaster

If that wasn't enough, Dualit even has eco-awareness on its side, as the toasters' ability to do one slice of toast at a time with a single plate means no electricity is wasted.

KITCHENAID'S PRO LINE TWO-SLICE TOASTER

Where? Many kitchenware stores and departments • www.kitchenaid.com • www.everythingkitchens.com

How Much? From $50

Desirability-wise, this brand is up there with the Dualit. As well as a pleasingly retro design, the Pro Line model has extra-wide and thick slots, so even real New York bagels will fit.

Towels

Hammacher Schlemmer

Where?
147 E. 57th St., between Lexington
and Third Avenues, N.Y.C. •
212.421.9000 •
www.hammacher.com

How much?
Bath towel $29.95

A selection of Turkish towels from Hammacher Schlemmer

What is it about fluffy white towels? Is it their cocooning quality? The super-luxe-factor? Or merely the fact that towels with a deep pile can dry you in next to no time at all—what bliss!

When it comes to quality control, towels are rather like sheets, rated by weight and provenance. Turkish-made are best, closely followed by Egyptian cotton. As for weight, the heavier they are, the deeper the pile, which makes them more effective as well as longer-lasting. Spend more, in other words, and your towels will be an investment in the long run.

Hammacher Schlemmer is a New York institution. Founded in 1848, the store has only ever had one mission: "To find quality." The result, thanks to their in-house institute, which researches and tests each of the products they sell, is the best the world has to offer. The towels sold here come from the Denizli region of Turkey, an area known for towelling of extraordinary thickness. They are 28oz in weight, the densest available, and with a ¼-inch pile that means they're very, very soft.

Designer Michael Kors swears by Hammacher's towels—and you know how fussy fashion folk are. "I love the minute when my white towels are no longer white, as it means that I can simply replace them with new ones," he says, and he admits to buying new towels every three weeks for his Fire Island summer house.

SCENES DE LIN

Where? 70 Rue de la Liberté, Marché du Guéliz, 4000, Marrakech, Morocco
How much? Prices from $9.75
This well-edited shop, the perfect escape from the heat, smell and dust of the souk, stocks everything a fabulously designed home could want, including giant hamam-style fringed towels. Hamam towels are generally rougher than most—all the better for a spot of exfoliation. Scenes de Lins' designs also look very stylish.

TERESA ALECRIM

Where? 76 Rua Nova do Almada, Lisbon, Portugal
How much? From $25
Portugal is a brilliant destination for bathroom gear—think fantastic-smelling soaps, cheap colognes, and fabulous towels. *Vogue* recommends Teresa Alecrim, a place that has been described as "Portugal's answer to Laura Ashley," for its embroidered monogrammed towels, a style popular in Lisbon.

Wallpaper

Florence Broadhurst

Where?
www.borderlinefabrics.com •
U.S. distributor: Classic Revivals, Boston •
617.574.9030 • www.classicrevivals.com

How much?
Upwards of $250 per roll.

We've voted Florence Broadhurst number one as her unique prints—bold designs that fuse metallic and tropical shades—have single-handedly spurred the current renaissance in wallpaper, convincing a younger paint-obsessed audience that it needn't be kitsch.

The Japanese Floral print, which features large flowers opened up like a fan, is regarded as her most iconic design, found in New York's branch of Soho House, for instance. It comes in a number of colors including silver, aubergine, lemon yellow and bright orange. Everything is made to order and all Broadhurst papers are screen-printed by hand. Other classic prints include Imperial Brocade, a new take on classic flock, Tiger Stripes, Horses Stampede, and Japanese Bamboo.

Originally from the Australian outback, Broadhurst spent some time living in Asia, where she founded an academy of modern arts, as well as Europe—she had a dress salon in Paris. After describing Australia as a "desert that likes to buy beige," she established a wallpaper studio. Broadhurst's flamboyant lifestyle made her a minor celebrity, but it was her company that gave her kudos—she continued creating two new designs a week until her death in 1977. "My success is the fact that my wallpapers have now become a status symbol," she once commented.

Florence Broadhurst's wallpapers lay forgotten until 1990, when her archive was discovered in a warehouse. The couple behind the discovery started a company—Signature Prints—and began distributing the designs across the globe. Today, the Signature Prints team works non-stop to satisfy demand. Some lucky homeowners in Sydney's more affluent suburbs still have original Broadhurst designs on their walls, while the Butterfly Room in the city's State Theatre sports a Broadhurst paper that now has protected status.

COLE & SON

Where? Lee Jofa, Inc. U.S./Mex.: 800.453.3563, Can.: 800.535.3258 • www.discountdecorator.com
How much? $100–$160 per roll
Exotic birds always make a popular print, and Hummingbirds from Cole & Son, a manufacturer with a royal warrant, manages to remain traditional, but not in the least bit boring. A classic.

TAPETTITALO

Where? www.tapettitalo.fi/english.html
How much? From $30 per roll
Tapettitalo is a Finnish company that makes some fantastic papers in prints that aren't commonplace—well, not yet. The Skylark design is their signature print, but Cherry Tree, a succession of cherry blossoms, is more subtle.

Jewelry

"It would be very glamorous to be reincarnated as a great big ring on Liz Taylor's finger."

Andy Warhol

Cufflinks

Longmire Stirrup cufflinks

Where?

10 New Bond St., London W1 •
www.longmire.co.uk

How much?

Plain white gold $3,400, with sapphires as shown, $13,000

For such a simple, practical accessory, it is still hard to find a truly stylish pair of cufflinks. The world seems full of tacky novelty varieties, which do a man's cuffs and credibility no good. Originating in the 19th century, cufflinks are a relatively new accessory for men, and glide between the practical and decorative—they are as useful as buttons, but double as fine pieces of jewelry. So, where do you go to find the best cufflinks a man can get? Straight to Longmire, the independent English jeweler that has long been producing fine and unique cufflinks— and holds that all-important royal warrant. Inspired by the Art Deco designs of the 1930s, the stirrup style has cut sapphires mounted in solid 18-carat white gold and wraps around the edge of the cuff. All very stylish indeed. The New Bond Street shop will also make a pair to your precise requirements.

Longmire Stirrup cufflinks

ASPREY 167 BUTTON PAVÉ

Where? 167 New Bond St., London W1 •
853 Madison Ave., N.Y.C., 212.688.1811 •
Beverly Hills Hotel, 9641 Sunset Blvd, L.A. •
www.asprey.com

How much? Evening cufflinks from $3,200

Asprey's 167-button pavé cufflinks are elegant and have just a hint of bling. But if this style doesn't tickle your fancy, don't worry, as Asprey's fine fleet of silversmiths and jewelers are available to carry out custom-made commissions.

Asprey 167 button pavé cufflinks

CARTIER

Where? 13, Rue de la Paix, Paris • Boutiques in N.Y.C., Honolulu, and dozens of other U.S. cities, plus Vancouver and Toronto • www.cartier.com

How much? From about $1800

The classic French jewelry brand specializes in diamonds, so its 18-carat yellow-gold cufflinks encrusted in the classic Cartier initials are utterly desirable.

Diamond ring

Wint & Kidd

Where?

237 Westbourne Grove, London W11 • The Courtyard, Royal Exchange, London EC3 • www.wintandkidd.com

How much?

Multi-colored diamond ring as shown. $39,900

In the 1944 Alfred Hitchcock film, *Lifeboat*, the star isn't the gorgeous, pouting Tallulah Bankhead; instead it's a glittering Cartier diamond bracelet. When a Nazi captain discovers the piece—left by Tallulah after her boat is bombed—he ponders: "They're really nothing but a few pieces of carbon."

Wint & Kidd

Men, eh? They just don't get diamonds. They don't understand how a little sparkle is good for the soul; how a pair of diamond studs can magically brighten the complexion; how a diamond—a real one, that is, not a manmade rock—is a miracle of nature, each one utterly unique; why diamonds are old-school glamor; and why they really are a girl's best friend.

Thank goodness, then, that diamonds are no longer the preserve of heirloom-fortuitous blue bloods. A combination of clever marketing, accessibility—cheap internet websites, for example www.cooldiamonds.com—and bling hip-hop stars means that the diamond market is now worth $60 billion a year, the highest it has ever been. This increased popularity has also meant an increase in awareness of the appalling mining conditions suffered by most diamond workers, and certain brands, which shall remain nameless, are targets of placard-heavy protests, a somewhat incongruous sight on the world's glitzier shopping streets.

Wint & Kidd are diamond dealers with a difference. Not only do they possess an almost unrivalled selection of colored diamonds—only one in 10,000 diamonds mined is colored—but the company also puts money back into Angola, where they source their stones, to house, feed, and educate street children. Wint & Kidd, in other words, is one of the few ethical faces in a trade riddled with human cruelty.

But ethics shouldn't be the only reason you choose Wint & Kidd. Their gem settings are discreet, making the most of the stone, something that is surprisingly rare in modern jewelry design, and they also make pieces to order. In addition, their shops, which are designed by Matthew Williamson, don't feel in the least bit mass-market, with helpful and knowledgeable staff on hand.

Their range of colored diamonds is exquisite. Colored diamonds are among some of the most valuable objects on Earth, their brilliant hues the result of impurities entering the stones as they form. The most rare are red, closely followed by green, purple, violet, orange, blue, pink, and yellow. Wint & Kidd stocks them all—as well, of course, as the more usual white.

HARRY WINSTON

Where? 718 Fifth Ave., N.Y.C., and stores in Bal Harbour, Honolulu, Beverly Hills and Las Vegas • www.harry-winston.com
How much? From $15,000

Established in 1932, the superstar jeweler is now synonymous with the Academy Awards—many an actress believes Winston baubles are lucky charms. Perfect if you're looking for household-name kudos combined with clever designs.

GRAFF

Where? N.Y.C., Palm Beach, Bal Harbour, Chicago, Las Vegas and selected Saks branches • www.graffdiamonds.com
How much? Engagement rings from $19,000

"The most fabulous jewels in the world," claim the diamond-specialists, a hyperbole that is, for once, not far off the mark.

Harry Winston ring

More important diamonds have passed through Graff than perhaps any other dealer, from the Star of America to the 137-carat Paragon. Graff is involved with the diamond at every stage, from the mining to the cutting and polishing, with workshops in the key diamond centres of Antwerp and Johannesburg. They specialize in pricey—but ineffably special—engagement rings.

DEALING IN DIAMONDS

The secret to clever diamond shopping is to understand the four Cs—carat, clarity, color and cut. Carat refers to the size of the diamond and clarity refers to the quality of the stone. As for the cut, there are a number to choose from: pear, round, marquise or princess, for instance; marquise and pear-shaped diamonds are the most flattering on shorter fingers. Uncut diamonds, which resemble pieces of unpolished glass, are also known as "rough diamonds," and are gaining popularity as a novel way to wear the stone. Really, what could be more decadent?

ROCK STARS

• The biggest diamond ever was the Cullinan, which was found in a South African mine in 1905 and weighed 3,106 carats (1.67lb) uncut. It was presented to King Edward VII as a birthday gift, who chose the Asscher brothers of Amsterdam as the cutters. It was a prestigious, if somewhat daunting, honor—when the initial split was performed, one of the brothers actually fainted from the stress. The Cullinan ended up as 105 stones, the brothers receiving 102 of them as payment. The two biggest, the Great Star and Lesser Star of Africa, became part of the British Crown Jewels. The pear-shaped 550.2-carat Great Star is still the largest polished diamond in the world, forming part of the Royal Sceptre.

• The Koh-i-Noor, a duck-egg shaped diamond that forms part of the British Crown Jewels, is the most famous of all diamonds. It is by no means the biggest diamond in the Tower of London; instead its fame derives from its tumultuous history. According to legend, the 600-carat diamond was discovered on the forehead of an abandoned child of the Hindu sun god on the banks of the Yamuna River. The gem passed from the Mughals to the Afghans to the Sikhs, several of its owners dying to protect it. A 6th-century valuation estimated that it was worth half the daily expenditure of the whole world. Then, in 1849, the British seized the stone and presented it to Queen Victoria. The monarch had a passion for gems and ordered the Koh-i-Noor to be cut and set into one of her crowns.

Gems

Gem Palace

Where?

M.I. Rd, Jaipur, India • branches in Mumbai, Agra, Udaipur, Delhi • Barneys in N.Y.C. & L.A. • Caribou Jewels, Aspen • www.gempalacejaipur.com

How much?

Prices on application

Rajasthan is *the* place for gem shopping and Jaipur its epicenter, in particular the shops along Haldion Ka Rasta and Gopalji da Rasta, near the Hawa Mahal. Here you'll find men cutting and polishing stones in dusty workshops, mostly for a made-to-measure market. For a more ordered environment, head to the Gem Palace and gasp at the bowlfuls of loose gems—rubies, emeralds, diamonds, opals, aquamarines, amethysts, tourmalines, and sapphires—displayed as casually as if they were candy.

Since 1852, the Kasliwal family has traded jewels to Indian royalty and celebrities like Mick Jagger, as well as European jewelry houses such as Bulgari and Cartier. Inside, the store is a veritable jewelry box. As well as loose stones, there are several ready-to-wear lines—the one by acclaimed Parisian jeweler Marie-Hélène de Taillac is especially recommended and targets

Loose gems

Western tastes. But the real joy here is going bespoke. Simple custom-made designs can be completed in a couple of hours. It is the Indian custom to buy stones by weight and then have them strung—the more complex designs are usually worked upon by the Kasliwal brothers themselves. The Gem Palace also sells exquisite antique jewelry.

BERGANZA

Where? 88-89 Hatton Garden, London EC1 • www.berganza.com

How much? From £500/$900

The key to finding great antique jewelry, as opposed in trawling around endless fairs, is discovering a dealer with a great eye. Berganza is such a shop: at the heart of London's jewelry quarter, the steady stream of ever-changing sparkling stock is delectable, with all important jewelry periods (Art Deco; Edwardian) amply covered.

FIONA KNAPP

Where? 178a Westbourne Grove, London • www.fionaknapp.com
How much? Prices from £800/$1,400

This New Zealand-born jeweler is relatively new on the scene, but she has already made a significant impact with bold designs that make the most of brightly hued stones—think pink sapphires and cerise tourmalines. Her pieces are future classics.

Oval mosaic aquamarine

Pink gold and pink sapphire Dandelion ring

Men's rubellite cufflinks

GLOBETROTTING GEM SHOPPING

Savvy shoppers buy their precious stones fresh from the mines, so knowing what comes from where is crucial.

Emeralds

Most come from South America, in particular Columbia. The best mines are in Muzo, Chivor, and Cosquez, and stones from these sites are a velvety, rich green. Bogota, the country's capital, is fast becoming the world's emerald marketing center. Brazil, Zimbabwe, Madagascar and Zambia, where the stones are an unusual bluish-green, are other rich sources.

Rubies

Rubies are the most valuable stone of all, and Mogok in Myanmar (Burma), an area that is known as the Valley of Rubies, is where you'll find the best in the world.

Gems

Museum and Gem Mark on Kaba Aye Pagoda Rd, also in Myanmar, are reliable local dealers. Many of these gems end up in Thailand, an important center for the ruby trade. The most prized shade is known as "pigeon's blood red," a color that is deep and rich.

Sapphires

These gems come in a variety of colors, including yellow and pink sapphires. A pink-orange coloring, which is known as a Padparadshah sapphire, is the most prized of all, closely followed by the cornflower-blue sapphires, which are found in Kashmir. Sri Lanka is the best place to go if you're looking for blue sapphires. Australia is currently the world's largest producer of sapphires, but these are not necessarily the prettiest—most are of an inky blue-black hue.

Gold

Garrard

Where?
202 N. Rodeo Drive, L.A. • 133 Spring St., N.Y.C. •
www.garrard.com

How much?
From $1,750 for a gold band

Dinh Van ring

Gold has been used in many different guises, from currency to crowns for teeth. It was first used by prehistoric man, and the oldest gold jewelry—discovered by archaeologists in the Sumerian Royal Tombs at Ur, now in Southern Iraq—is thought to date back to around 3000 B.C. At about the same time, the ancient Egyptians were beating gold into leaf, as well as alloying it with other metals. In 1352 B.C., the young Egyptian King, Tutankhamen, was interred in a pyramid tomb laden with gold, his remains placed in an extravagant gold anthropoid sarcophagus. When the tomb was opened, it revealed an incredible 2,448 lb. gold coffin and hundreds of gold and gold-leafed objects.

So what are the origins of the gold wedding band? Dating back to Egyptian times and also used by the Romans, the ring is thought to simply resemble life and eternity. But it wasn't always so glamorous; wedding bands were simply iron hoops until the second century AD, when the true beauty, luster, and resistance of gold was fully realized.

Dating back to 1722, when original founder George Wickes entered Goldsmiths Hall, Garrard is most famous for making royal crowns. Now, with Jade Jagger at the helm, the luxury jeweler has managed to step into the 21st century and is without doubt one of the most glamorous places to go for a classic gold wedding band.

DINH VAN
Where? 15, Rue de la Paix, Paris • jewelers in 13 U.S. cities • www.dinhvan.com
How much? From about $450 for a wedding band
Vietnamese-born, Paris-raised goldsmith, Jean Dinh Van, worked for Cartier in the 1950s and 1960s and now produces some of the most exquisite and luxurious gold designs in the world. The gold bands are gorgeous.

ME & RO
Where? 241 Elizabeth St., N.Y.C. • 61 E. Oak, Chicago • 1901 Collins, Miami • 8405 Melrose Place, L.A. •
www.meandrojewelry.com
How much? From $205 for a 10-carat lotus gold pendant, 18-carat pendants from $825
Hip New York-based designers, Michele Quan and Robin Renzi, create pretty modern bracelets and necklaces.

Gold for less

Istanbul, India and Greece are just a few of the countries where you can find beautifully designed gold on the cheap. In Greece, A. Patrikiadou is notable for selling excellent Byzantine jewelry dating back as far as the 4th century B.C. Istanbul is brilliant for buying intricately designed gold at very reasonable prices—it is just a matter of haggling a bit here and there, while Tribhovandas Bhimji Zaveri in Mumbai, India, has five floors of gold and gems to riffle through. (A. Patrikiadou, 58 Pandrossou, Athens, Greece; Tribhovandas Bhimji Zaveri, 241-43 Zaveri Bazaar, Mumbai, India.)

Pearls

Mikimoto

Mikimoto

Where?

730 Fifth Ave., N.Y.C. • The Venetian, Las Vegas • 3333 Bristol St, Costa Mesa • Beverly Wilshire, L.A. • Chateau d'Ivoire, Montreal • Joseph Anthony, Windsor • Jubilee, Ottawa • www.mikimotoamerica.com

How much?

Cultured pearl 16-inch single strand with 7x6.5-mm pearls, and gold clasp $2,300

Pearl devotees are as classy as they come: think Coco Chanel and the long strings that decorated her black bouclé suits, Audrey Hepburn in *Breakfast at Tiffany's* and the Queen of England. An essential element to any jewelry box, a good set will make an outfit. But what makes a good set?

Only about one per cent of all pearls are natural. These true pearls, a beauty born of irritation, are known as "oriental pearls" and come from mollusks known as pearl oysters, found mainly in the Persian Gulf, Red Sea, and the Gulf of Manaar, between India and Sri Lanka. An irritant enters the oyster and is then surrounded with thin layers of nacre, or mother-of-pearl (a protein consisting of calcium) until a pearl has been formed. Cultured pearls result from induced irritation in farmed oysters.

Mikimoto provides the best cultured-pearl necklaces, primarily because they leave the oysters alone in the nacre-building stage for the longest. Kokichi Mikimoto, the son of a noodle restaurant owner, acquired a patent for the pearl-culturing process in the early 1900s. Since then, the label has farmed Akoya pearl oysters, assisting the conception, letting the oysters grow for two years, and then inserting a mother-of-pearl bead into the shell. The oyster is then left for at least a further two years, during which time the nacre should have built up.

A velvety pink luster makes a pearl highly prized. The perfect pearl should have a smooth, unblemished skin. A good quality-control test is to use your teeth—proper pearls should feel gritty when passed against them.

A single strand is the most elegant; more strands—à la Coco Chanel—are good for the evening. Regular wear is good for pearls; they gain luster from contact with oils found in the skin. No excuse then, so get on your pearls, girls!

TIFFANY & CO.

Where? 727 Fifth Ave., N.Y.C. • 85 Bloor St. W., Toronto • Check www.tiffany.com for other Tiffany locations

How much? From U.S.$175 for a single cultured-pearl necklace

Recently, this world-famous jeweler has adopted the "something besides diamonds" approach, and introduced a small collection of pearl pieces. Expect fresh, clean, modern designs.

> **"You can turn an absolute whore into a lady by just putting pearls round her neck."**
>
> Donald Brooks, costume designer

SOUTH SEA PEARLS

Where? Specialized outfits, for example www.pearlparadise.com

How much? Several thousand dollars per pearl

Along with Tahitian examples, these natural pearls are the best—and the biggest at more than 10mm (½in) in diameter. They are found in silver, black, and gold.

Silver jewelry

Georg Jensen

Where?

4 Amagertorv, Copenhagen • Georg Jensen stores in Manhattan, Short Hills, NJ,
Greenwich, CT, Chicago, Las Vegas, L.A., Honolulu • www.georgjensen.com/english

How much?

From $190

Georg Jensen founded his silversmithy in Copenhagen in 1904 and quickly became known for his fine silver wares and cutlery. Simple, distinctive, and strikingly modern, the 100-year-old Danish company is still easily one of the most collectable silver brands around—in fact, there's an entire website dedicated to Georg Jensen antiques (www.georgjensenantiques.com). Today, Jensen's "Home" collection is as equally sought-after as his jewellery.

Georg Jensen bangle

Georg Jensen ring

Georg Jensen earrings

TIFFANY & CO.

Where? See p.120 for locations • www.tiffany.com
How much? Heart tag bracelet is $175—engraving is extra
Established in New York in 1837 and famous for adorning Audrey Hepburn in the classic film *Breakfast at Tiffany's*, Tiffany & Co. remains one of the world's most glamorous silversmiths and is known for its sterling silver "Heart Tag" charm bracelet.

ROBERT LEE MORRIS

Where? 400 West Broadway, N.Y.C. • 212.431.9405 • www.robertleemorris.com • retailers throughout the U.S.
How much? Petit Cross earrings, $95
If you are looking for something a little more rock 'n' roll, seek out the bold and geometric shapes of this award-winning contemporary designer. We're addicted to his cute silver stud earrings.

Simply Charming

The charm bracelet is possibly one of the most alluring and oldest forms of jewelry—Cowrie-shell bracelets date back thousands of years, and were worn to promote fertility and wealth.

Today, the charm bracelet is most commonly designed in silver, and Tiffany & Co's (www.tiffany.com) heart-shaped sterling silver "Heart Tag" has become one of the world's most iconic. Links of London (www.linksoflondon.com), which has stores on Madison Ave. and on West Broadway, N.Y.C., offers infinite variations which can be customized.

Along with silver sculptures and desk accessories, Zimbabwean artist Patrick Mavros (www.patrickmavros.com) creates the cutest charm bracelets featuring tiny silver animals, including lions and rhinos. We're totally smitten.

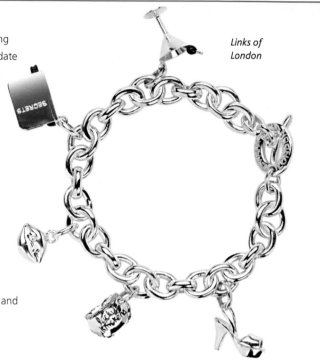

Links of London

EXPERT SILVERSMITH AND SILVER SCULPTOR, PATRICK MAVROS, GIVES THE LOW-DOWN ON SILVER SHOPPING:

How is silver different in attitude to gold?
Patrick Mavros: "Silver is less formal, yet designed and crafted wisely it can be transformed into something more spectacular than the yellow metal. Silver is softer to look at and is often more flattering on a face or wrist than gold."

Where does the best silver quality originate?
PM: "Pure silver, otherwise known as fine silver, has the same quality around the world, yet the richest reefs of ore are found in the ancient mines of Central and South America."

Are there different grades of silver?
PM: "Fine silver is alloyed with copper to give it strength. The end result is sterling silver. Other alloys are used depending on whether the silver will be used for enamelling or soldering."

How can you tell if silver is of a superior quality?
PM: "Silver must have an even, lustrous surface, with no porosity marks—these look like bubbles or stain-like blemishes. Hallmarks, the most visible sign of all, will tell you if silver is sterling or not."

How do you clean silver?
PM: "Most pieces of jewelry can be cleaned by rubbing them gently with a silver cleaning-cloth. These cloths are obtainable from most jewelers or stores that have silver departments. Some silver dipping solutions are also excellent cleaners. Just remember to rinse your jewelry afterwards with clean water. Silver foam can also be used."

Watch for men

Omega Seamaster Planet Ocean Big Size

Where?
329 North Rodeo Drive, L.A. • Carried by many dozen watch sellers in U.S. and Canada • www.omegawatches.com

How much?
From $2,500

Rolex Oyster Perpetual Submariner

Selling impeccably-made pocket-watches when it was established in Switzerland in 1848, Omega soon became synonymous with the most reliable watches in the early 20th century. Simple, sturdy and blessed with the ultimate seal of approval, that of Mr. Bond (yes, Daniel Craig wore one in *Casino Royale*), the Omega Seamaster is a real-deal man's watch. Fashioned in steel on a rubber strap, practicality is key with this design: it's water resistant to 600 metres (well, you never know) and features a domed, scratch-resistant, sapphire crystal front.

ROLEX OYSTER

Where? Rolex dealers worldwide • www.rolex.com • www.amazon.com
How much? From $3,500
The legendary Swiss watchmaker was founded by German businessman Hans Wilsdorf in 1905. Innovations have included the self-winding watch, which was introduced in 1931 and is powered by an internal mechanism that uses the movement of the wearer's arm. All 220 of its components are assembled by hand.

BREITLING BENTLEY 6.75

Where? www.breitling.com
How much? From $5,500
Oozing masculinity, this chunky hunk of a watch resembles the engine of the impressive Bentley Arnage limousine that inspired its design. The Breitling was originally designed for aviation use, as the extra-large face provides good visibility.

*Breitling
Bentley 6.75*

A SHORT HISTORY OF TIMEKEEPING

Measurements of time were initially based on observations of seasonal cycles, while shorter intervals were measured by observing the shadow cast by an upright object, such as a sundial. Then came the hourglass, followed by the "clepsydra," a water clock that measured the flow of liquid from a container. The earliest watches were ornate and date back to the 1500s, but the first mechanical, machine-made watches were invented as late as the 1850s. The first modern-looking wristwatch evolved in the 1900s, although pocket watches were still popular until the Second World War, when servicemen found wristwatches more practical. Although the digital watch was invented in the 1960s, it is the classic Swiss-made dial watch that reigns as the most elegant timepiece.

Watch for women

Hermès Cape Cod

Where?

24 Fanborg Saint-Honore, Paris, plus 23 other French cities • 691 Madison Ave., N.Y.C., plus 15 other U.S. locations • 755 Bar Barrard St., Vancouver • 131 Bloor St., Toronto • www.hermes.com

How much?

$1,600

The elegant double leather strap in classic tan or black and simple, rectangular face with a plain gold or silver frame makes this one of the most wearable and desirable watches in existence. Ineffably chic.

CARTIER TANKISSME

Where? 13 Rue de la Paix, Paris • 653 Fifth Ave., N.Y.C. • www.cartier.com • www.amazon.com

How much? From $14,000

Founded in 1847 by Parisian Louis-François Cartier, the company, which is known for its diamond-studded designs, first opened a London boutique in 1902. The 18-carat-gold, diamond-set Tankissme watch (pictured on page 113) is timelessly elegant with a small square face, diamond edging and chunky white-gold silver links.

EBEL BELUGA LADY

Where? Tourneau stores in North America • website lists dealers: www.ebel.com

How much? $10,000 plus

Established in Switzerland in 1911, this luxury watch brand creates the ultimate "jewelry" watches. The sleek and elegant "Beluga" is set with gems—which can include diamonds, if you wish.

Hermès Cape Cod

AND THE AWARD FOR MOST EXPENSIVE WATCHMAKER EVER...

Goes to Vacheron Constantin, a Swiss company founded in 1755, which became famous for its intricate skeleton-style watches in which the wearer can see all the inner workings. The Kallista watch, named after the Greek word for "most wonderful," was made from gold ingot and set with over 130 carats of emerald-cut diamonds. It took 8,700 hours to make and sold for over seven million dollars.

Shoes & accessories

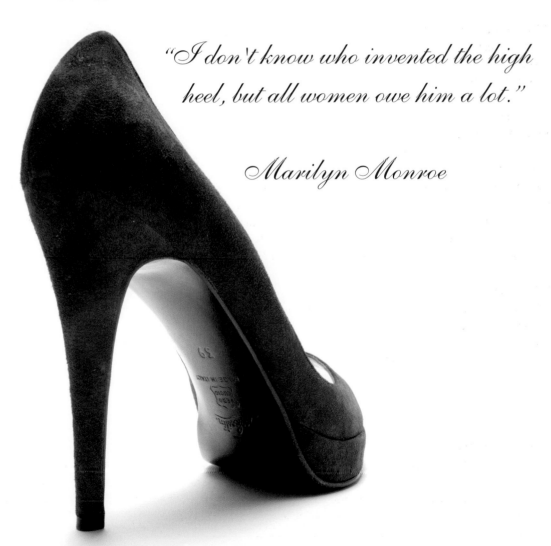

"I don't know who invented the high heel, but all women owe him a lot."

Marilyn Monroe

Belt

Gucci GG clasp green-red-green belt

Where?
Gucci stores in U.S. and Canada • www.gucci.com
How much?
$285

Whether it's ultra-wide, super-skinny, studded or embossed, a well-made leather belt can transform a look in one easy fastening of its clasp. And if there's one belt that transcends styles, trends, and eras, it is Gucci's classic GG belt in the brand's signature green-red-green color. Produced by craftsmen in Tuscany, this belt was worn by supermodels and entrepreneurs in the 1980s, preppy rich American kids in the 1990s, and suave Italians since the very beginning. It epitomizes a cool, laid-back luxury. You can wear it dressed-down with jeans and a tight T-shirt, or up with a prim pencil skirt and towering heels. The message: expensive, thoroughly grown-up and properly put-together.

Gucci

HERMÈS H-CLASP BELT

Where? 24 Rue du Faubourg St. Honoré, 75008, Paris • 691 Madison Ave. N.Y.C. • other Hermes shops in U.S. and in Montreal, Toronto and Vancouver • www.hermes.com
How much?
U.S.$435

What exactly is it about that sleek golden H? The classic Hermès leather belt has become a passport to instant chic. Just sling it round a pair of skinny jeans, a slim skirt or over mannish tailored trousers, and it will add instant style and polish.

BOTTEGA VENETA WOVEN LEATHER BELT

Where? Bottega Veneta stores worldwide • www.bottegaveneta.com • www.net-a-porter.com
How much? $490

This classic Italian brand is famed for its high-quality lattice-woven leather, producing some of the most desirable belts in the world. Each belt is hand-tooled in Italy using the softest nappa leather known to man and woman.

Brogues

John Lobb

Where?

9 St James's St., London • 680 Madison Ave., N.Y.C. and six other U.S. cities •
www.johnlobb.com

How much?

Bespoke Oxfords from $3500

No other shoe has such classic appeal as a pair of finely crafted leather Oxfords, and nobody does them quite like John Lobb. Established in 1866, when Lobb designed a smart pair of riding boots for the Prince of Wales and was promptly awarded a royal warrant, the brand has since become a favorite with numerous well-heeled business men and celebrities, including Cecil Beaton, Somerset Maugham and, more recently, Hugh Grant and Prince Charles, all of whom appreciate the classic style and superior craftsmanship. Lobb also crafts loafers and riding boots.

John Lobb

Each Lobb pair is made from the finest leather, which is cut to the anatomical dimensions of the feet, while invisible details like full-grain leather insoles, linings, and stiffeners add to the comfort of the shoes. The bespoke service at the elegant, wood-panelled London store is impeccable, and starts off with a measurement by a fitter, who then makes up a wooden last of your foot. A "clicker" helps decide on the exact leather, taking into consideration your requirements, and then sends the details to the company's Northampton factory, where the shoes are hand-sewn. It is an involved process and, depending on the style of the shoes and leather required, takes varying amounts of time; one of the most unusual leathers is alligator, which can take up to four skins—and three months—to ensure consistency in the grain and texture.

The most flattering brogue is Lobb's simple punched-toecap Oxford, the Philip II style. A mighty fine shoe and an investment for life, provided that you treat them with T.L.C.

BERLUTI

Where? 2 Rue du Pont-Neuf, 75001, Paris • 971 Madison Ave., N.Y.C. • Barneys • www.berluti.com
How much? From $1,300
Berluti was established by an Italian woodmaker in Paris in 1895, and make sleek, refined shoes and low boots with a distinctly Continental aesthetic.

CHURCH'S

Where? 201 Regent St., London W1 • Church's English Shoes, 689 Madison Ave., N.Y.C. • D.C. and Houston stores • www.styledrops.com • www.solelyshoes.com
How much? From $295
A traditional British brand, specializing in good-quality ready-to-wear leather Oxfords.

" Always use a shoehorn—it will help to keep your shoes in perfect shape. Walk your new shoes in gradually, wearing them for no more than a few hours, and in dry conditions for the first few days. This allows the leather to soften, and better fit your foot-shape. Rotate your pairs of shoes, so that they can dry out and breathe. If wet, leave your shoes to dry out naturally (never use an artificial heat source) on their sides so that air can circulate around both the upper and the sole. Generally, shoes will last longer if cared for properly and cleaned regularly."

Andres Hernandez, Production Manager

at John Lobb

John Lobb

Clutch bag

Lulu Guinness fan

Where?
3 Ellis St., London SW1 • 394 Bleecker St., N.Y.C. • www.luluguinness.com
How much?
From £395/$790

*"**B**are shoulders are a must for evening dresses and having a shoulder strap spoils the line, this is why a clutch bag is so good. As an accessories designer, I always make the bag the biggest statement of the outfit and shoes should complement but they certainly don't have to match. The worst look is when a woman wears a pale evening dress with a heavy dark quilted bag."*

Lulu Guinness

It is neither the most fashion-forward nor the most dazzling of clutch bags, but it is the most collectable, classic, and utterly desirable, adored by glamazons that include Jemima Khan, Halle Berry and Sophie Dahl. Lulu Guinness's clutch fan combines humor with elegance, and a dash of vintage glamor, reminiscent of old-style Hollywood. The British bag designer, who started her label in 1989 with a simple briefcase for ladies containing a bright suede lining, designed her first "fan" bag in 1995, which subsequently sold out. Cleverly, Guinness only makes a limited number of bags, so each one becomes that much more unique and desirable. The "fan" is a statement in its own right—you can wear the simplest of little black dresses and the elegant design will add a large dose of glamor and grace.

Lulu Guinness

JUDITH LEIBER MINAUDIERE CRYSTAL CLUTCH

Where? Leiber boutiques in Atlanta, Las Vegas, Costa Mesa •
outlets in Woodbury Common (Hudson Valley) and Desert Hills
(Palm Springs) • 680 Madison Ave., N.Y.C. • www.judithleiber.com
How much? From $1,895

When Renée, Nicole, and Scarlett are wondering which bag to
take with them to their next red carpet event, there's no hesitation:
a Judith Leiber minaudiere. Leiber's exquisite and expensive,
gem-encrusted hard-case clutch bags spell all-out glamor.

VBH'S SATIN ENVELOP CLUTCH BAG

Where? www.net-a-porter.com
How much? $670

Rome-based and Florence-produced label, VBH (the initials of owner,
V. Bruce Hoeksema, who used to work for Valentino) run a range of
simple-but-striking envelope clutches that have acquired something
of a cult following. Each bag is individually handcrafted and sewn
by an intimate team in Florence, using the finest leathers. The
signature rhodium-plated clasp makes this bag even more special.

*Judith Leiber
minaudiere crystal
clutch, green*

WHERE TO BAG A VINTAGE CLUTCH

Until Coco Chanel invented the handbag in 1929,
the clutch ruled supreme as the elegant choice for
carting your compact, lipstick, and other essentials
around. This means there are lots of 1920s (and earlier)
clutches tfor vintage fiends to find—it's just a matter of
knowing where to look. In London, there are some
fabulous vintage bags stalls and accessory shops full of
great clutches, including Alfies Antique market
(www.alfiesantiques.com) and Portobello Market. In
Paris, head to the flea market at Porte de Cligancourt
(officially called Puces de Saint-Ouen), where you'll find
clutch bags galore, dating back to the late 19th
century. In Hollywood, go straight to Jet Rag (825 N.
La Brea Ave), in Manhattan, head for Cherry (19 Eighth
Ave) for the cream of the clutch crop.

Cowboy boots

Texas Traditions

Where?
2222 College Ave., Austin, Texas •
512.443.4447 • TexasTrad@aol.com
How much?
From $400

For the wannabe, like *Midnight Cowboy*'s Joe Buck, the allure of a finely crafted pair of cowboy boots is practically narcotic. Dating back to mid-19th century Texas, the first cowboy boots were developed with a sturdy Cuban-style heel to grip in the stirrup. It wasn't until the 1920s that cowboy boots became a fashion accessory thanks to a number of fictional cowboy characters on the radio. The increased popularity of Western movies and the men who starred in them from the 1940s onwards—particularly the likes of John Wayne—only deepened the appeal of these boots. They've been in and out of fashion ever since—worn by stars as diverse as Lenny Kravitz, John Travolta or Tom Cruise, and more recently by female fashion icons like Sienna Miller (who popularized them with her modern bohemian look), Joss Stone and Britney Spears.

Texas Traditions

So, if you are an absolute cowboy boot fiend—and, let's face it, you either love them or loathe them—where do you go to find the best of the best? The answer is Texas Traditions, a company dating back over a hundred years. In 1937 it famously produced the most valuable cowboy boots ever; studded with diamonds, rubies, and gold, they were designed for a high-profile gambler. Now owned by Lee Miller, who took over from Charlie Dunn, Texas Traditions still makes the best quality handcrafted leather cowboy boots in the world, which is why all the top country singers—and Sting—won't go anywhere else.

TONY LAMA
Where? Henry Beguelin, 18 Ninth Ave., at 13 St, inside Hotel Gansevoort, N.Y.C. • Stores throughout U.S. • www.tonylama.com • www.cavenders.com • www.bootbarn.com
How much? From about $120
A hundred production stages go into making a Tony Lama boot, which is constructed to fit a wide variety of sizes in a selection of skins that range from calf to ostrich. Each boot features a shank, a heavy gauge double-ribbed steel strip that supports the arch, and is made to survive the rugged toughness of the high desert terrain around El Paso, where they are still handmade. Boots for men, women and kids.

Eyeglasses

Frédéric Beausoleil

Where?
5 Bis Rue de l'Asile Popincourt • Better opticians and eyewear shops everywhere • www.beausoleil-sunglasses.com • www.eyewearselect.com • Dreyfus Opticians, Yardley, PA (dreyfusopticians.com)

How much?
From $275

With the advent of laser surgery and contact lenses, wearing specs has become a little like listening to vinyl or using a fountain pen: an antiquated quirk that's not entirely necessary. Still, the die-hard spec wearer knows that a good pair of glasses can say a lot about image, appearance and status. Sure, there are modern alternatives, but somehow that takes the fun away from glasses, which are one of the few fashion accessories to fuse science with fashion, and simultaneously symbolize intellectualism and professionalism. But where should you go for the ultimate pair?

Trained by an old spectacle manufacturer in Paris, Frédéric Beausoleil set out to design the most perfect glasses in the world. His label was established in 1987, and since then he's been selling his quality handmade frames to the likes of Al Pacino, Penelope Cruz and Julia Roberts, all of whom love his finely crafted signature rectangular frames.

GOLD & WOOD

Where? Josephson Opticians, 60 Bloor St. W., Toronto • Optical Illusions, 378 Santana Row, San Jose • Contacts and Specs, 3144 W. Broadway, Chicago (www.contactsandspecs.com) • www.gold-and-wood.com

How much? From $600
Maurice Leonard started making frames from fine wood in the early 1990s. In 1997, the Luxembourg designer revived the rimless look, and in 2001 he introduced the Bijoux collection, which includes indulgent solid-gold frames inlaid with gemstones.

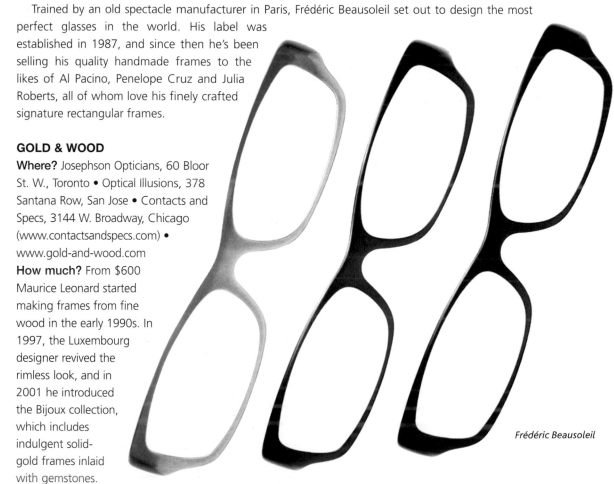

Frédéric Beausoleil

Alain Mikli's Starkeyes spectacles

ALAIN MIKLI STARKEYES

Where? 4 Rue Bachaumont, 75002, Paris, • 575 Madison Ave. and 968 Madison Ave., N.Y.C. • www.mikli.com • www.eyeglasses.com

How much? From $350

While not to everybody's taste, the thick, bold frames of Alain Mikli are instantly recognizable, and spell confidence and style. His recent collaborations with designer Philippe Starck make for some of the most desirable specs going, due to the fact that they are resistant to air and water corrosion, twice as light as titanium, and three-times lighter than steel.

THE WORLD'S BEST EYE BOUTIQUES

Adam Simmonds
87 Regents Park Rd., London
www.adamsimmonds.co.uk

Anne et Valentin
4 Rue Sainte Croix de la Bretonnerie, Paris
www.anneetvalentin.com

Facial Index
1F Mitsubishi Denki Building, 2-2-3 Marunouchi, Chiyoda-ku, Tokyo, Japan

Isis
153 Fulham Rd., London

Michel Guillon
35 Duke of York Square, Sloane St., London
www.michelguillon.com

Niche Optical Tailor Ltd
119 Canleriggs, Glasgow, Scotland

Robert Marc
575 Madison Ave. and 5 other locales, N.Y.C.

AND WEBSITES...
www.klasik.org
www.olivergoldsmith.com
www.retrospecs.co.uk: you can commission the same style of specs Audrey Hepburn wore in the 1966 film, *How to Steal a Million*

Fountain Pen

Mont Blanc Meisterstück 149

Where?

www.montblanc-us.com • 18 Neuer Wall, Hamburg, Germany • 181 Bloor St., Toronto • Cherry Creek Mall, Denver • Penn Square Mall, Oklahoma City • Palace Hotel, King St., Charleston • 232 Plaza Frontenac St., St Louis • two dozen other Mont Blanc boutiques in the U.S. • www.refills.montblanc.com

How much?

About $500

Mont Blanc Meisterstück 149

The Mont Blanc Solitaire Royal pen, which is encrusted with 4,810 diamonds, is the most expensive pen ever at $125,000. Of course there are far cheaper alternatives—but Mont Blanc remains the brand with the most cachet.

The company was founded in Germany in 1906, and was innovative from the start, making special fountain pens with blades instead of nibs for architects and engineers during the 1920s. But its most popular style is the Meisterstück, in particular the chubby, cigar-shaped 149 model. The pen is utterly iconic and instantly recognizable—so much so that it is now on permanent display at New York's Museum of Modern Art. The Meisterstück was first introduced in 1924, and famous users include JFK and most of the recent Popes.

Made of black resin with a gold trim, the cap is topped with a signature Mont Blanc white star, a motif that represents the snow-covered summit of Mont Blanc itself. The nib is equally special, made from 18 carat gold with a platinum inlay. Each 149 passes through the hands of 120 people during its three-month production process, which includes checking the sound it makes when it hits paper. Mont Blanc has resolutely resisted the urge to use cartridges and so pens must still be filled with ink from a bottle.

The torpedo size might feel unwieldy in smaller hands; thankfully, the Meisterstück also comes in smaller sizes, all made with the same design values—the "Classique" is a popular example. When pen shopping, you should try as many styles as possible to discover which you find most comfortable.

PARKER 51

Where? Vintage pen specialists, including: Cajun Pen Shop, Metaire, L.A. • www.vintagepens.com • www.fountainpenhospital.com • www.parker51.com
How much? Depending on color, date, cap style, and condition, from $100

Everyone from the composer Puccini to thousands of school children the world over has used a Parker pen. The most covetable model of this American brand is the Parker 51, introduced in 1941; like the Mont Blanc Meisterstück, it can be found in New York's Museum of Modern Art.

> "**My** two fingers on a typewriter have never connected with my brain. My hand on a pen does. A fountain pen, of course. Ballpoint pens are only good for filling out forms on a plane."
>
> Graham Greene

DUPONT ORPHEO

Where? 58 Avenue Montaigne, Paris • www.st-dupont.com • www.paradisepen.com • www.inkflow.com
How much? From $575

Perhaps the most elegant line on the market, France's answer to Mont Blanc uses lush Chinese lacquers to coat their pens. Their limited editions are well worth seeking out.

Gloves

Madova

Where?

Via Guicciardini, Florence, Italy • www.madova.com

How much?

From $46

A smart pair of leather gloves is the best way to finish off a winter coat. A family firm that was founded in Florence in 1919, Madova claims to be the only shop in Europe, and quite possibly the world, that sells and produces leather gloves—and nothing else.

Madova's strong point is variety—visit the shop and you can find a glove in virtually every color under the sun, at any length, both unlined and lined in wool, silk, cashmere, and the warmest—albeit least animal-friendly—rabbit fur. Helpful assistants will find you the correct size; new gloves should be tight-fitting as they'll stretch with the shape of your hand. The staff will also present you with a handy booklet detailing tips on how to care for and clean your gloves. For the ultimate in glove luxury, plump for the made-to-measure option, which is also surprisingly affordable—around $60 for kidskin leather lined with silk.

Madova

AGNELLE

Where? www.agnelle.com • Galeries Lafayette, 40 Blvd, Hausmann, Paris • (sometimes) Bergdorf Goodman, N.Y.C. • (sometimes) www.leatherglovesonline.com

How much? From $140

This Paris-based company makes gloves for Louis Vuitton, Christian Dior, Lanvin, and Celine, as well as producing its own line. Best known for stylish designs with a twist—think tassel details and bows resting on the wrist.

PICKETT

Where? 32–33 and 41 Burlington Arcade, London • www.pickett.co.uk

How much? From £19/$38

Pickett is best for gloves in bold colors. Particularly recommended are the gentlemen's cape leather "Officers" gloves, with delicious details such as a red silk lining and a button fastening on the wrist.

Handbag

Hermès Birkin

Where?
Hermès stores worldwide • www.hermes.com
How much?
From $6000

Right now having a designer handbag is more important than possessing a designer dress—the "it" bag is the fashion phenomenon of the 21st century. And while the world's chicest women will happily shop at Zara for clothes, there's no way they'll compromise when it comes to their bags—they must be as covetable and lust-worthy as can be. If there's one bag that outshines the competition, it is the Hermès Birkin. Loved by Kate Moss, Madonna and Elle MacPherson alike, it still garners waiting lists of three months or more. The actress, Jane Birkin, inspired the creation of the first of these bags in 1984—a supple, large black leather carry-all, which knocked the Kelly from the top spot. Now available in a variety of different sizes, including the popular shoulder style, which features a longer handle, the Birkin can be ordered in 8,000 different combinations of leather and fastenings. The most exclusive and expensive bags are crocodile. A Birkin, customized with a clasp and lock, featuring 14 carats of pavé diamonds set in white gold, recently sold at Doyle's auction in New York for a cool $64,800. If you want one, remortgage your house now.

Hermès Birkin

Chanel 2.55

CHANEL 2.55
Where? Chanel boutiques • Neiman Marcus • www.chanel.com
How much? From $1,400
It was 1929 when Coco Chanel first designed the shoulder bag; until then the clutch had ruled as the choice of elegant handbag for women, and soldiers' satchels were the only bags with straps. Chanel declared: "I tired of carrying my bag in my hand and losing it, so one day I added a strap and wore it as a shoulder bag."

By 1955, she'd developed a quilted chain-strap bag, now referred to affectionately as the "quilt and guilt."

MULBERRY BAYSWATER

Where? 605 Madison Ave., N.Y.C. • 387 Bleecker, N.Y.C. • Pier Shops at Caesars, Atlantic City • 8407 Melrose Place, L.A. • selected Barneys, Neiman, Nordstrom and Saks

How much? $900

This leather holdall became an instant hit when it was developed in 2003. The brand was established in the 1970s by Roger Saul and has become something of a cult bag label ever since. Luella Bartley hooked up with Mulberry in 2001 to create the famous Gisele bag. Mulberry, and its roomy Bayswater handbag, will go down as an all-time classic.

Mulberry Bayswater

A SHORT HISTORY OF THE "IT" BAG

1932 Louis Vuitton Noé In signature monogram canvas, this was one of the very first cult handbags, thanks to its practical drawstring and elegant strap.

1944 LL Bean Tote Before fridges were commonly used, LL Bean in Maine introduced the Ice Carrier made from heavy duty canvas. It was renamed the Boat & Tote in the 1960s as it became increasingly fashionable.

1958 Hermès Kelly Bag A hit when it launched in the late 1950s, this Hermès bag was renamed after Grace Kelly when she carried it around throughout her engagement to Prince Rainier. The Kelly still garners three-month long waiting lists.

1965 Gucci's "Jackie" Shoulder Bag Simple in shape: a curved leather body with a Gucci clasp and curved shoulder strap, this bag fits snugly under the arm, and became the must-have bag of the 1960s.

1996 Hervé Chapelier Travelbags These French holdalls with signature contrasting interior and exterior waterproof nylon canvas became a fashion statement during the mid to late 1990s.

1993 Kate Spade Tote The most simple of concepts: a durable, simple-shaped nylon tote that became one of the most unlikely—and bestselling—American accessory style hits in the 1990s.

1999 Fendi Baguette A frenzy began soon after Fendi launched its now legendary baguette bag in the late 1990s. The fight was on to find ever new and more embellished versions, whether mirrored, sequin-scattered or appliquéd.

2002 Luella Gisele In simple tan, this satchel-inspired bag with buckles and straps became an instant best seller for Mulberry. Luella then launched many new variations on the theme under her own label, Luella. These came in different shapes and colors, including bubble-gum pink.

2003 Balenciaga City Motocycle This neat handheld leather bag's defining feature was its wispy leather tassles. Kate Moss carried hers everywhere she went for a while; her patronage helped to propel it to the height of style stardom.

2005 Chloê Paddington The slouchy leather bag with its signature weighty gold padlock shot to the top of the must-have bag super league the moment it was launched. A more compact version soon followed.

2007 Goyard Uber-ubiquitous designer bags are supposedly passé, replaced by more anonymous carry-alls by the likes of French label Goyard. So guess what's become the new must-have trophy bag? Why, Goyard's, of course, the supposedly anonymous anti-It-Bag, a point illustrated when the *New York Times*' Bill Cunningham devoted an entire page to Manhattanites he'd snapped trotting out with the identikit tote. Plus ça change.

Luggage

Louis Vuitton

Where?
Louis Vuitton stores worldwide • www.louisvuitton.com • www.eluxury.com
How much?
From $850

The two most important jobs of a suitcase? First, to hold your clothes neatly and safely, and second to look so refined that you will have fellow travellers drooling in the baggage reclaim hall. There is no contest when choosing which will garner the biggest drools: a Louis Vuitton classic monogrammed trunk. The label, established in 1854 with the creation of its flat trunk (which remains the classiest style) has been selling its Damier canvases since 1888, and the iconic monogrammed canvas since 1896, to the super rich from Posh and Becks to British royalty. But what, exactly, is the attraction with these cases? Perhaps the simplicity of the logo? The subdued gold and brown color? Or the chic gold clasps? It is probably a combination of all three, but there is no doubt about it: Vuitton's classic LV monogrammed canvas trunks are the most luxurious, expensive, and, let's face it, ostentatious, luggage sets in the world.

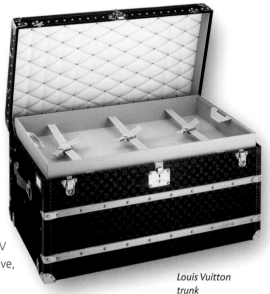

Louis Vuitton trunk

GLOBE TROTTER

Where? 54–55 Burlington Arcade, London • Barneys New York •
For bespoke cases, email bespoke@globe-trotterltd.com
How much? From $299
Established in 1897, the Globe Trotter, with its old-fashioned charm, is the archetypal English suitcase. They are made from Vulcan Fibre, a unique, patented material that is as light as aluminium but as hardwearing as the finest leather, and thus rather brilliantly last a lifetime. Each piece is lovingly hand-crafted at the company's Hertfordshire factory by the same machines that were used in the early 1900s. Globe Trotter now offers a bespoke service that invites clients to choose from a selection of colors, exclusive Liberty-print linings, contrasting leather corners, and personalized initialling.

Globe Trotter customized suitcase

Goyard Palace trunk

GOYARD'S PALACE TRUNK

Where? 233 rue St Honoré, Paris, France • 345 Powell St., San Fransisco, Barneys, Bergdorf Goodman

How much? From $6,000

Goyard was established by Françoise Goyard in 1853, a year before Louis Vuitton. The exquisite French company became the most sought after trunk maker in the late 19th century. Francoise's son, Edmond, styled the coated canvas covering with the iconic hand-painted chevron design featuring the distinctive type: Goyard Saint Honoré. Today, the original values, attention to detail and fine craftsmanship remain—each piece of luggage is still made from poplar wood, leather, fabric, and beech with clasps and handles in nickel, bronze, and jewels. The finishing flourish is a signature hand-painted motif which can be easily customized with the initials of those willing to pay for it.

HOW TO PACK WITHOUT CREASING: GARRY CHARNOCK, BRAND MANAGER FOR JEEVES OF BELGRAVIA (WWW.JEEVESOFBELGRAVIA.CO.UK)

• "How you fold your garments is very important. Make sure that you fold your clothes around the body pulse points—believe it or not the body heat generated around the bend of the knee, the wrists, and elbows will help steam out the creases in your items when you wear them.

• Pack shoes toe to heel in the bags they arrive in.

• Jersey—do not fold, just roll, and then unravel for minimum creasing (this will also act as a stabilizer to fill any spaces).

• Pleated skirts and dresses—twist the pleat and pull it into a stocking to maintain the pleat.

• Double bag all cosmetics to avoid spillage in your suitcase. Ideally, take all your cosmetics in a vanity case to protect them from damage.

• Always take laundry bags.

• Take a large canvas holdall if you intend to shop."

Flats

Repetto

Where?
22 Rue de la Paix, Paris, France • Noisette, Brooklyn, NY.• Jildor, Southampton, NY • Barneys• Sabot, Atlanta • Tula, Chicago• Gimme Shoes, Rabat, S.F.• Bind L.A. • www.shoefly.com

How much?
From $145

Repetto flats

Remember that famous image in *Working Girl* of Melanie Griffith dashing through Manhattan's financial district in an 'eighties power skirt suit teamed with sneakers? A couple of years ago, the ballerina flat ballet slipper replaced the sneaker as the comfort shoe of choice – not to say the laidback evening alternative to the stiletto. The best are from Repetto, purveyors of Parisian ballerina style. Launched in 1947 by Rose Repetto – after her choreographer son urged her to start a boutique specializing in dancewear—the shoes soon picked up a following. After Brigitte Bardot wore a pair in *And God Created Woman*, Repettos were transformed into a wardrobe staple – the most quintessential being the stitched-returned style, which has a leather sole sewn into the shoe inside out before being turned the right way round, ensuring the fit is super-tight (and subtly sexy). Repetto has done pop-up stores with Ernest Sewn and been part of a Comme des Garcons collection. For aspiring Amélies everywhere.

FRENCH SOLE
Where? 985 Lexington Ave., N.Y.C. • Bloomingdales • Saks • www.zappos.com
How much? From $98
The world's largest collection of ballet shoes, the company claims—and who are we to argue? When speaking strictly of dance shoes, however, Capezio might take issue. Some French soles (which are actually English) verge on the frumpy—for example, the quilted, but most are classics with toe cleavage a go-go.

MARC BY MARC JACOBS
Where? Company boutiques in Provincetown, MA; Savannah, GA; S.F.; L.A.; N.Y.C.; Las Vegas; Chicago; Boston • JonesNewYork • www.shopbop.com
How much? From $150
Less obvious than Chanel's double-C flats, Marc skimmers are great for fashion-forward wallflowers (the kind of girls Jacobs prefers). Most styles include a small heel—more flattering than no heel at all. Available in a fabric — from tweed to rubber—to suit every taste.

Sandals

K Jacques

Where?
25 Rue Allard, Saint Tropez •
Saks Fifth Ave. • www.kjacques.fr •
www.shopbop.com

How much?
From $208

K Jacques

Sandals may be the simplest form of footwear, but there's a huge difference between the kind you buy for $5 from a cart vendor and the hand-tooled leather variety, which are properly fitted to your feet and can be found in Europe's most exclusive resorts. The ideal sandal should transport you from beach to cocktail party; it should be elegant, yet practical, and show your feet off in the best possible way—complementing a tan and distracting attention from chubby chipolata toes.

The most famous and adored sandal shop in the world, the K Jacques store in St Tropez, was established in 1933 by Monsieur and Madame Jacques Kéklikian. It was a shrewd business move: in St Tropez, sandals are as much a necessity as jeans and a white T-shirt. Their new style of made-to-measure sandals swiftly granted them a celebrity following, and in the 1960s the shop shod the soles of Brigitte Bardot. Today the firm is still a family business, and has three sales outlets in St Tropez, as well as a showroom that creates sandals for a wide range of the world's leading designers, including Karl Lagerfeld, Missoni, and Helmut Lang. With a choice of over 200 styles, you can get any shape, style or color made up with a special bespoke service that takes just a few hours. The only additional requirement is an immaculate pedicure.

AMEDEO CANFORA "JASMINE" JEWELED THONG

Where? 3 Via Camerelle, near Piazzetta Quisisana, Capri, Italy • www.canfora.com

How much? From €175/$275, sandal shown $345

Founded by Amedo Canfora in 1946, this company is now looked after by his daughters Angela and Rita. Situated on the glitzy Italian island of Capri, this sandal shop dishes out elegant sandals to well-dressed holiday makers, from models to fashion designers, all of whom adore the handmade, jeweled, thong designs. Elegant, glamorous and distinctly Italian.

*Amedeo Canfora
"Jasmine"
jewelled thong*

STAVROS MELISSINOS "SOPHIA LOREN" LEATHER CORD SANDALS

Where? Melissinos Art, 2 Aghias Theklas, Athens • www.melissinos-art.com

How much? From $27–$35 depending on size, plus $13 shipping

A poet and sandal maker who has been tooling both words and leather for more than 50 years, Melissinos has made shoes for both Sophia Loren and the Beatles. His 15 types of sandal can be adjusted to fit as you wait.

Scarf

Duchamp

Where?
Barneys • Holt Renfrew • www.duchamplondon.com
How much?
From $120

Men's scarves have a huge and varied history: they are evident on ancient Chinese sculptures; the Romans later wore something called a sudarium, which was a linen kerchief; and in 17th-century Britain, no man would be seen dead without an elegant silk scarf. Widening and protecting the neck, it was considered to reinforce masculinity and was adopted by women much later on. Recently the silk scarf has made something of a comeback, along with bespoke suits, brogues, and silk socks. A silk scarf is gentlemanly, luxurious, and a sign of total refinement. Duchamp men's accessory label has a selection of the most delightful gentleman's silk scarves in vibrant prints and colors.

ETRO

Where? 720 Madison Ave., N.Y.C., and shops in Miami, L.A., and Las Vegas • www.etro.it
How much? From $200
The Italian fashion brand famous for its colorful paisley prints does fine silk scarves for men, including colored pashminas that are as dapper as can be.

Duchamp

Slippers

Pia Wallén

Where?
www.peekkeep.com • www.piawallen.com
How much?
$60–$75

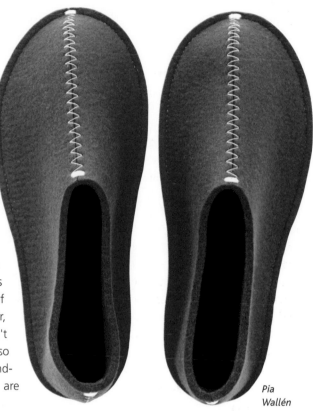

Pia Wallén

Coming from a place where it's dark most of the year, the Scandinavians know a thing or two about comfort. They also know a thing or two about style, making Pia Wallén's wool felt slippers the best when it comes to keeping your toes toasty.

Wallén is an award-winning Stockholm-based interior designer who started working in high-quality felt—and never really wavered. Her slippers are made from just that, with contrasting zig-zag stitching across the toe and rubber soles, available in a number of pleasingly bright colors and styles. The full-footed affair, for instance, is perfect for the kind of people who don't want their slippers to look like, well, slippers. Wallén also makes a range of rugs, blankets, pillows—her hand-woven wool throws with a cross motif, "The Crux," are now classics.

And while we're on the subject of slipper shopping in chilly climates, super-warm Mongolian slip-ons made from yak leather and camel hair also come highly recommended.

BELDI BABOUCHES

Where? Beldi, 9–11 Souikat Leksour, Medina, Marrakech, Morocco
How much? $75
Moroccan babouches are *the* smart slipper choice. The pointy-toed version was invented in the Moroccan city of Fez, where distinctive yellow and white slippers are still made today for the royal household. Those with a rounder toe - less severe and more aesthetically pleasing - are from Marrakech, the smartest from Beldi, a boutique that flawlessly blends oriental craftsmanship with occidental taste. Beldi's babouches are more expensive than most but worth it since they're hand-sewn in the finest leather. Jean Paul Gaultier is a fan—he has a riad in the old medina—as are many of his fellow fashion jetsetters.

UGG SHEARLING SCUFFS

Where? Neiman Marcus • diverse local retailers • www.amazon.com • www.zappas.com
How much? $59–$75
From the same brain that brought you the Ugg boot, scuffs are crafted from soft suede with a toe-pleasing sheepskin lining. Perfect for chilly winter's nights when only sheepskin will do.

Socks

Pantherella

Where?
Better men's departments and clothiers • www.dann-online.com • www.onthefly.com
How much?
From $50 per pair

For many men, socks are something of a trademark. Think about it: how else are they going to stand out from the corporate crowd? Pantherella has been going for over 65 years and is generally considered the best sock-maker in the world—if you're buying your suit from Savile Row, Pantherella is your sock. Keep an eye open—this small luxury occasionally appears at discounters, such as Marshalls or T.K. Max.

Pantherella

The company's founder, Louis Goldschmidt, established a fine-gauge knitting plant after spotting a trend towards lightweight clothing. Even today, Pantherella insists on using only the highest-quality yarns—cashmere, silk and merino wool, for instance, as well as its bestselling line in Sea Island cotton. Pantherella has exclusive rights to make socks from genuine Sea Island cotton, so, unlike "Sea Island quality," which is used by many of its competitors, this is the real deal—it's as strong as silk, as soft as cashmere, and as long-lasting as wool; cool in summer, warm in winter.

Pantherella's other claim to fame is the socks' hand-linked toe seam, a skilled process that other sock manufacturers have rejected as too expensive. The process creates an invisible toe seam, which means increased comfort for the wearer. As for the correct sock etiquette, Savile Row tailors decree that no skin should be shown between the sock and trouser leg when sitting down.

BURLINGTON ARGYLE SOCKS

Where? Department stores
How much? Approximately $12

Burlington make the best brightly colored argyle socks, which come complete with trademark stud. They're so good, in fact, that the 13th Duke of Argyle starred in one of their advertising campaigns—the diamond pattern is based on the Argyle tartan.

GAMMARELLI

Where? Via dei Cestari, Rome
How much? Approximately $15

This shop is known as "the Pope's couturier," as the boutique, which was established in 1798, has dressed virtually every Pope since then. It is best for bright cardinal-red socks, which are ribbed and come to the knee—some men have a fetish about such things. Also available in Archbishop Purple.

Stilettos

Manolo Blahnik

Where?
31 W. 54 St., N.Y.C. • Wynn, Las
Vegas • Neiman Marcus •
www.footcandyshoes.com

How much?
From $690

Manolo Blahnik

Madonna once described Manolo Blahnik's shoes as "better than sex," adding "what's more, they last longer." She has a point. In an average lifetime, a woman spends up to three years of her life shopping, shelling out more than $40,000 on shoes. Is it any wonder, then, that the search for the perfect pair of stilettos is so vital?

Manolo Blahnik is a man who knows all about this and his shoes have become legendary for their ability to turn a woman into a sex siren within seconds of stepping into them. Blahnik, who was born to a Spanish mother and Czech father, and raised on a banana plantation in the Canary Islands, studied literature at the University of Geneva, and art at the École du Louvre in Paris. During a trip to New York, he had an appointment with the then editor of *Vogue*, Diana Vreeland, who encouraged him to settle in London and set up his shoe label.

A QUICK Q&A WITH MANOLO BLAHNIK

Why does a stiletto heel change the way a woman looks so dramatically?
Manolo Blahnik: I adore the way a woman's body changes when she puts on heels; it is an instant transformation, no surgery necessary! From a technical point of view, when you raise the heel it forces the body to work completely differently.

How does it alter her attitude?
MB: Shoes are always instant theater, they help a person act who they want to be.

When is a strap good? Any rules?
MB: Every single woman's legs are completely different, and luckily there are endless options for straps. As a rule, an ankle strap will cut your leg, making it appear shorter, so if your legs are proportionately short, I would advise against straps. Each person must try everything on to find what works best for them.

When should stilettos be worn?
MB: ALWAYS!

When shouldn't stilettos be worn?
MB: If you are visiting an apartment or house with exquisite 18th-century parquet flooring.

Your first memory of stilettos?
MB: Possibly my mother in shoes of her own design.

Your favorite stiletto wearer of all time and why?
MB: Women in general!

It is lucky for the women of the world that he did. From the outset of his career, Blahnik has had an instinct for proportion that has placed him above his competitors; his stilettos miraculously lengthen the leg from the hip right down to the tip of the toe, and his classic shapes and styles are never overtly fashionable, remaining timelessly stylish. And while every celebrity from Nicole Kidman to Kylie Minogue has stepped out in a pair of Manolos, it is good old Marge Simpson, who wore a pair of his mules during a 1991 episode of *The Simpsons*, and, of course, *Sex and the City*'s Carrie Bradshaw, who symbolize exactly how culturally significant Manolo stilettos really are.

Manolo Blahnik

Christian Louboutin

CHRISTIAN LOUBOUTIN

Where? 941 Madison Ave., 59 Horatio St., N.Y.C. • Shoe departments in top stores • www.bluefly.com

How much? From $560

This French designer is known for his slim, vertiginous pencil-like heels with signature Chinese-red soles that have prompted men to follow women down the street upon seeing a flash of scarlet. Louboutin, who was inspired to become a shoe designer at the age of ten after spying a woman in an art gallery wearing the most striking pair of heels, says his shoes are "a worktool or a weapon and an objet d'art." As well as producing two collections of drop-dead sexy shoes a year, he works on private commissions—love letters and locks of hair are among the things that have been encased in those spiky, conical, wicked heels of his.

A shoe-a-holic website

www.shoewawa.com is one go-to website for shoe lovers, covering news on the latest brands and styles, as well as the newest eBay offerings so you know all about that must-have pair of Manolos or Ferragamo Mary-Janes selling for pennies. It also features many specialist categories, including "ugly shoes," "design classics" and "wedges." Fun for shoe-addicts everywhere.

HISTORY OF THE STILETTO

The inventive shoe designer, Salvatore Ferragamo, created the reinforced steel bar that gave rise to the stiletto heel in the 1950s. But it was French shoe designer Roger Vivier who took it one step further in the following decades, fully realizing the potential of the stiletto as an iconic heel shape. The stiletto heel is now one of the most stylish and important heel shapes in existence, and features not only in exclusive designer shoe collections, but on Main Street, too.

Stilettos with a twist

Olivia Morris sets trends with her quirky shoe adornments, from polka-dot prints to silk bows. www.oliviamorrisshoes.com

Georgina Goodman of London has become known for her well-made, cone-shaped, wooden stacked heels in supple leathers; she also offers a semi-bespoke service. www.georginagoodman.com

Rupert Sanderson's elegant heels with a dash of old-fashioned frivolity are continually accruing fans, including modern-day sex siren Scarlett Johansson.

Bruno Frisoni has worked with Christian Lacroix and Jean-Louis Scherrer. This Paris-based shoe designer is inspired by the 1960s, cinema, and pop music.
24 Rue de Grenelle, Paris
www.designerexposure.com

Azzedine Alaia Tunisian-born fashion designer Azzedine Alaia became known for his strict, body-hugging clothes in the 1980s. His imposing, powerful and sexually charged heels remain at the height of cool. Available at www.shoebunny.com.

Pierre Hardy

PIERRE HARDY

Where? 156 Galerie de Valois, Paris • Holt Renfrew • Mona Moore in Montreal • Barneys • www.pierrehardy.com • see website for more U.S. locations

How much? From about $700

After designing shoes for Hermès, Pierre Hardy launched his own collection in 1999. Hardy fast became identifiable for his super-sleek vertiginous heels, sculptural shapes and beautifully crafted uppers. In Paris, he is considered the king of the cobbling craft. In 2008, he did sandals for GAP that sold for under $100.

Sunglasses

Ray-Ban

Where?
Almost everywhere you look.
How much?
From $100

More than merely functional, sunglasses signify status, wealth, and, above all else, image. One of the most iconic styles is the classic Ray-Ban Aviator. Army Air Corps commissioned Bausch & Lamb to design the teardrop-shaped Aviator in 1936 out of necessity—pilots had been suffering from headaches and nausea because of glare and the great distances they needed to travel. The name Ray-Ban was chosen for the new product to emphasize the fact that the eyewear could "ban" or block out the sun's rays and protect the wearer's eyes. In 1952, Ray-Ban launched a new model, the Wayfarer, a style that was promptly snapped up by Hollywood stars, including Audrey Hepburn, who wore a pair in *Breakfast at Tiffany's*. The Aviator was popularized again in the 1980s, when Tom Cruise wore them in *Top Gun*. To this day, Ray-Bans, recently enjoying a renaissance, remain timeless.

Ray-Ban

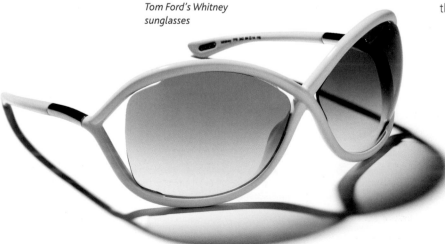

Tom Ford's Whitney sunglasses

TOM FORD
Where? 845 Madison Ave., N.Y.C. • www. brandnewsunglasses.com
How much? From $240
Not long after quitting as Creative Director of Yves Saint Laurent, Tom Ford, the king of high-octane fashion, launched Tom Ford

Oliver Peoples' Harlot sunglasses

Eyewear. His sunglasses collection, with its streamlined, sleek, and look-at-me styles, gained instant credibility among the world's fashion fiends.

OLIVER PEOPLES' CAMEO

Where? www.oliverpeoples.com/shop • Oliver Peoples stores in the U.S. and Japan • Selected opticians worldwide

How much? Glasses shown: $340

A striking, 70s-inspired style, Oliver Peoples' Harlot comes in a selection of shades, including bubble-gum pink, olive tortoiseshell, and ultra-sophisticated mahogany brown. The L.A. brand, established in 1986, has fast become favored by celebrities, including Kate Moss, who has made them famous by wearing the black version non-stop. Oliver Peoples has serious rock and roll credentials.

Say it with shades

- **Bottega Veneta:** For Milanese-style chic.
- **Chanel:** If only because of those tiny interlocking Cs on each side.
- **Dior:** Heir- and heiress-glamor, think Paris Hilton.
- **Roberto Cavalli:** The choice of the linebacker and his wife for maximum show.
- **Yves Saint Laurent:** Refined with a dash of opulence.

WHICH STYLES SUIT WHICH FACE SHAPES BY TOP OPTOMETRIST, MICHEL GUILLON

- **Round (soft, no angular features).**
  Go for: contrast by adding feature: rectangular/hexagonal frames.

- **Rectangular (marked and more balanced features, as a square face, but not as wide).**
  Go for: softer shape, oval to soften the image.

- **Triangular (like a rectangular face but with narrow chin).**
  Go for: small non-angular eye shape to minimize the difference in head width between the eye region and chin.

- **Square (broad face with strong jaw and chin).**
  Go for: rectangular elliptical frame with rounded softer corners.

- **Oval (soft regular features).**
  Go for: the choice is yours, with any style you wish: discreet to minimize contrast or bold to maximize impact.

Sneakers

Adidas Superstar

Where?
Sports stores worldwide •
www.adidas.com •
www.shoebuy.com
How much?
From $69

Adidas Superstar

Without doubt, the most iconic trainer or sneaker is the Adidas Superstar. This model first went on sale in 1970, and recently celebrated its 35th anniversary. Initially worn by NBA players, it fast transcended to the street. In 1986, U.S. hip-hop band, Run DMC, released the track "My Adidas" and threw away the laces. There's something almost personable about the chubby round toe, the short, smart shoe shape and the thick laces that make it aesthetically appealing and as comfy as can be.

Nike Air Max 90s

NIKE AIR MAX 90S
Where? www.nike.com •
Selected sports stores worldwide
How much? From $90

One of Nike's two founders, Phil Knight, was a middle-distance runner at the University of Oregon and established Nike in the early 1970s, naming it after the Greek winged goddess. The brand, which was the first to launch the clever concept of limited editions, came up with the Air Max design in 1987—it displayed the all-important air bubble sole prominently, and became a cult-classic in 1988 with this sleek and simple design. The Air Max continues to be re-released in updated versions each season.

REEBOK CLASSICS
Where? http://store.reebok.com •
Selected sports stores worldwide
How much? From $40

"Let's put on our Classics and have a little dance shall we?" sings The Streets' Mike Skinner, the recent face of Reebok Classics. So what's the draw of these athletic shoes? Simple lines, mostly white and unpretentious in shape and style, the Reebok Classic has an urban coolness that has made it the choice for many on both sides of the pond. Their strength is the simplicity of design, which makes them so easy to wear and classic.

Reebok Classics

Umbrella

Swaine Adeney Brigg

Where?
54 St. James, London • www.englishhall.com •
Sterling & Burke, D.C. (1.800.205.7739) •
www.classicluggage.com

How much?
From $195

*Swaine
Adeney Brigg*

For the discerning gentleman, an umbrella is not just for keeping the rain off, but is a telling status symbol. Umbrellas may have been used in China and India for thousands of years before they ended up in England in the 18th century, but there's no doubt that the U.K. is now home to the best-quality umbrellas in the world. Swaine Adeney Brigg is as old-fashioned a company as they come. Originating in 1836, it has been making umbrellas for the British royal family ever since. Its history is diverse, supplying luggage to Rolls Royce, Aston Martin, and Bentley, and bullwhips for Indiana Jones in *Raiders of the Lost Ark*.

When it comes to umbrellas, the company's signature pieces include the Brigg Malacca umbrella handle, fashioned from Malaysian Mallaca cane, but the ultimate in luxury is the ebonized wood umbrella. There is also a ladies' parasol with a rhino horn handle, a snip at just $2100. You wouldn't want to be leaving that on the subway now, would you?

JAMES SMITH & SONS

Where? 53 New Oxford St., London, WC1 • www.james-smith.co.uk
How much? From $190

James Smith & Sons has been a shrine to the umbrella since the 1850s. There is a bespoke service that allows you to choose the wood and color you desire, as well as measuring the umbrella so that it is the right length when you walk. The elegant rosewood style is a fine-looking specimen.

*James Smith
& Sons*

Budget "brollies"

If the thought of spending hundreds of dollars on an umbrella makes you sweat, go for a more practical foldaway option. A telltale sign of a good umbrella is the quality and quantity of rivets in the frame—make sure there are lots of them, and that they are secure and well-made. One of the best foldaway umbrellas is the Knirp Duomatic Fiber T1. It features a carbonfibre frame, and it is rust-proof and apparently storm-proof. It is available at James Smith & Sons (see above) for about $130.

Wallet

Connolly

Where?
Connolly, 41 Conduit St., London
How much?
From $198

Connolly

A wallet is one of the most practical and important accessories there is: where else can you put all those platinum credit cards and cash? If you're looking for a suitably stylish wallet, then look no further than Connolly, the quintessentially English luxury brand that is famous for its fine quality leather goods. Connolly has produced some of the world's best leather, which has been used on the first ever Rolls Royce, Edward VII's coronation coach, Concorde, and the QE2. The company dates back some 200 years, when James Connolly built a small business as a tyresmith. Since then Connolly leather has been used to fashion the boots of British soldiers in the First World War, on the seats on London buses, on the first tube trains, and in approximately 14 parliaments around the world, including the Palace of Westminster. No wonder Ralph Lauren is a huge fan.

MULBERRY

Where? 387 Bleecker St., N.Y.C. •
see p. 137 for other store locations
How much? $300

Mulberry

Another great British brand, Mulberry produces some of the most desirable leather accessories in the world, including its classic faux tortoise-skin leather wallets. The company was established in the 1970s in rural Somerset, where it remains today, and still employs local craftsmen and artisans. The accessories marry style and function, so they not only look good but feel great too. The classic wallet features an ample slot for four credit cards, a coin section, two hidden compartments, and a cash sleeve.

GOYARD

Where? 233 Rue Saint Honoré, Paris • 345 Powell St., S.F. • Barneys • Bergdorf Goodman • Holt Renfrew • www.goyard.fr
How much? From $800

Believe it or not, this French luxury luggage brand, established in 1853, was once bigger than Louis Vuitton and was the first of the two companies to introduce coated canvas printed with its signature pattern—it still produces fabulous steamer trunks, by the way. A wallet with the classic Goyard chevrons, which are always hand-painted on, is a subtle sign of style. An insider's secret.

Leisure

"They talk of the dignity of work.
The dignity is in leisure."

Herman Melville

Bicycle

Pashley Princess Sovereign

Where?
Pashley Cycles, Stratford-upon-Avon, England • www.pashley.co.uk • www.eurocosm.com
How much?
£540/$875

Invented by Thomas Humber in 1868, bicycles are bound up in childhood memories: we all remember the first time the training wheels came off and the joy of pedalling freely. Buying a bicycle is in many ways a more personal and sentimental process than buying a car or a scooter. And while there are thousands of high-tech, super-modern bikes in all sorts of shapes and sizes, none has the romance, history or aesthetic delights of William Pashley's elegant and traditional ladies' bicycles. Lovingly handmade for over 70 years in Stratford-upon-Avon, this quintessentially English bicycle features a front basket, five-speed alloy hub gears, and a Brooks leather saddle with springs that mold to your bottom. The Princess Sovereign, available in Regency Green, Buckingham Black, or Rich Burgundy, is stylish, classic, and a pleasure to ride.

Pashley Princess Sovereign

SCHWINN CRUISERS

Where? Most bicycle stores and many sporting goods stores • www.schwinnbike.com
How much? From $299
Founded in the United States in 1895, Schwinn was one of the original purveyors of the modern bicycle. The company has since brought us many classic bikes, including the stylized Sting-Ray—with its high-rise handlebars, "banana" seat, and enlarged back wheel—in 1963, and the BMX in 1970. Its fabulously lightweight Whitewall Typhoon cruiser tire is the original smooth roller for easy riding, featuring corrosion-resistant alloy wheels, and stainless-steel spokes. The Cruiser has classic, curvy, 1950s' styling, and a two-tone color.

CANNONDALE JUDGE DOWNHILL/FREERIDE BIKE

Where? www.cannondale.com
How much? From $5,000
Available in three models, this awesome mountain bike has state-of-the-art suspension and super-sporty aesthetic. The 6061 twin triangle mainframe has gone through over a hundred fatigue, impact and strength tests to ensure that it's as durable and high-performing as can be. The Judge is for serious mountain-biking enthusiasts who like to test their cycles to the limits.

Camera

Leica MP

Where?
www.leica-camera.com •
Various outlets worldwide
How much?
About $4,000

Leica MP

The digital age is upon us, with pundits predicting that film will soon be a thing of the past. Leica aficionados beg to differ, believing that these are the only cameras worth hanging round your neck, thanks to an unusually quiet shutter release, a commanding ability to take excellent pictures in even the gloomiest of light, and, of course, handsome good looks. With a Leica you must wind the film on and learn how to use a rangefinder—a separate viewfinder and focusing device. All these niggling idiosyncrasies are part of the reason why Leicas are so well-loved.

The German company has been making cameras since 1925 and actually invented 35-mm photography. Leicas entered photography mythology when Henri Cartier-Bresson, who was never seen without his Leica, buried his camera when he thought he was going to be captured during the Second World War.

The MP was launched in 1956, and models from the 1950s and 1960s are now highly collectable. It was cleverly relaunched in 2003, and the company went on to sell more cameras than it had since 1968. The MP model is still made by hand and, of course, includes a Leica lens—said to be the best. There is even an "à la carte" service that allows Leica lovers to custom-build their camera; choices include Hermès calfskin. The Leica is even easy to repair; indeed the company guarantees that new owners will be able to get hold of parts for their camera for at least 30 years after purchasing, something refreshing in a disposable oonsumer culture such as ours. No wonder people like Leica a lot.

> " **T**he Leica has timeless styling, a classic form and always produces the very highest quality images."
> **Sir Paul Smith, British designer and keen photographer**

CONTAX T2
Where? From second-hand camera dealers, or try online sellers such as eBay
How much? The price varies, but expect to pay $400–$600
This discontinued camera is still the off-duty choice of many a fashion photographer—Mario Testino claims he carries one at all times. Indeed, in recent years the Contax T2 has been used increasingly in professional shoots, with Terry Richardson and Juergen Teller (he uses one for those iconic Marc Jacobs ads) among its fans. Professionals love the "verité" this point-and-shoot can produce. A cult choice.

LOMO
Where? www.lomography.com • http://shop.lomography.com • www.amazon.com
How much? $50–$75 for a Colorsplash model
This cult Russian camera comes with a simple philosophy: "Don't think, shoot." The contemporary idea behind these cheap cameras, originally mass-produced during the Soviet era, is to take as many pictures as possible. The often unpredictable results mean a user can create a piece of art—even the kind of photograph it would take other photographers days to set up. Alternatively, he or she could have a blurred mess. Either way, it's experimental.

Classic car

Aston Martin DB5

Where?
www.classic-british-cars.com •
www.classiccarsforsale.co.uk •
Classic car dealers
How much?
Price varies

Aston Martin DB5

Cars have become one of the most pioneering and designed objects of the modern age, and are now among the most state-of-the-art, technologically exciting purchases you can make. But nothing carries quite the same kudos as a classic car. A symbol of style, class, and utter refinement, a beautifully designed old-fashioned motor will garner raised eyebrows from across the street and—quite literally—stop traffic.

If there is one classic car that reigns high above the rest in terms of cool and good looks, it is a Bond car. The sleek and curvaceous Aston Martin DB5 is the one Sean Connery famously drove in *Goldfinger*—although his was equipped with machine guns, bulletproof shields, ejector seat, and revolving licence plates. Founded in the U.K. by Lionel Martin and Robert Bamford in 1914, Aston Martin soon made a name for itself by making zippy racing cars, producing several for the French Grand Prix in the 1920s. In 1947, the company was bought by Sir David Brown—who gave his initials to the series to which the DB5 belongs. Only 886 of these cars were ever built, so you'll have to look long and hard if you want one, although you could, of course, opt for another model in the DB range. To this day, an exceptional level of workmanship goes into each Aston Martin produced. A classic, stylish, and thoroughly refined choice.

JAGUAR E-TYPE

Where? www.jaguar-e-type.net • www.web-cars.com • www.eaglegb.com • Classic car dealers
How much? From around $40,000–$80,000 for an E-Type Roadster in good shape.
Also known as the E-type or XK-E, this magnificent car was designed by Malcolm Sayer, an aerodynamics engineer, and is distinctive due to its elongated bonnet, and sleek, airplane-like structure. The fact that it could reach 150mph (241km/h) and cost half the price of its competitors when it was launched in 1963 caused a sensation. Sayer claimed it was the first car to be "mathematically designed." It was also the first sports car to be mass-produced—over 70,000 were built, which means it should be possible to track down a second-hand model within a few months. Then again, you can always opt for Jaguar's new take on the E-type, complete with a sleek, leather interior, control console with switches, and baritone exhaust.

VOLVO P1800

Where? volvo1800pictures.com • www.volvocars.us • www.cardomain.com
How much? About $10,000
Yes it's a Volvo, the Swedish car manufacturers known for their angular and practical cars, but the P1800 also happens to be the company's coolest model. It shot to fame in the 1960s, after appearing as Roger Moore's preferred mode of transport in *The Saint*, and possesses a robust engine, an aerodynamic look, and stylized fins. Less showy than a Bentley or Merc—a hip and affordable option indeed.

Golf driver

TaylorMade R7

Where?
Better golf and club shops • www.taylormadegolf.com
How much?
$300-$400

> **"G**olf is a game that is played on a five-inch course—the distance between your ears."
>
> Bobby Jones, legendary golfer

A driver has been described as "the club that separate contenders from the pretenders." It is also the most expensive club in the bag, something that should also include a variety of woods, irons, a pitching wedge and a putter—golf rules allow a maximum of 14 clubs.

A driver is what a golfer uses to whack the ball when he or she tees-off—"drive for show, putt for dough," so the saying goes—and male players, in particular, are obsessed with the length of their tees. The TaylorMade R7 is truly revolutionary. A driver that's currently most popular with professionals, as well as amateurs who can afford it, it is so prized, in fact, that many professional players use this brand for no financial reward.

The TaylorMade brand is renowned for its innovative use of new technology, and the R7 is no different, made up of a series of weights that can be adjusted with a special wrench to six different "launch settings." It is illegal to walk around a course adjusting the head of your clubs; instead, you set the driver to work around your weaknesses. When the R7 was first introduced a couple of years ago, it astounded the golf world. TaylorMade has since conceded that the R7 has a 95 per cent satisfaction rating and quite rightly describe it as "the most highly awarded driver in the world."

The company was started in Illinois in 1979 after the founder, Gary Adams, discovered balls struck by metal drivers travelled much further than those struck by traditional woods. Other brands worth buying for your bag include Titleist and Ping.

TaylorMade R7

CALLAWAY HYPER X TITANIUM
Where? Better golf shops • www.callawaygolf.com
How much? $300–$360
The number-one selling brand in the United States (TaylorMade is number two), this driver is a mix of titanium and carbon, excellent for power and precision.

CLEVELAND LAUNCHER
Where? www.clevelandgolf.com • www.clickandsavegolf.com • Golf and sporting goods shops
How much? From $250
A model with a big titanium head, this is the perfect driver for those with a high handicap.

Scooter

Vespa GTS250

Vespa GTS250

Where?
Vespa dealers • U.S.: www.vintagevespascooters.com • Canada: www.vespacanada.com

How much?
Approximately $5,750

Vepsa is Italian for "wasp"—and if you've ever heard one of these scooters zipping down a street, you'll know why. The vehicle was invented by Rinaldo Piaggio as the perfect cheap vehicle to get Italy moving again in the postwar period. He instructed his designers to create a scooter that was suitable for both men and women, could take a passenger and wouldn't get clothes dirty—crucial for fashion-conscious Italians.

The first Vespa was introduced in Italy in 1946 and was an immediate success, since it proved so skilled on the country's bomb-scarred roads. Since then, Vespa has sold more than 16 million scooters worldwide and notable models include the LX, made famous by Audrey Hepburn in the movie *Roman Holiday*, and the ET2, which arrived on the scene in 1996 and helped invigorate sales in urban areas (this is the model Gwyneth Paltrow rides).

The GTS250 is the latest and most powerful Vespa yet, and is an updated version of the GS (the Grand Sport), a model that is on permanent display at the Museum of Modern Art in New York. The GTS250 has Vespa's trademark rounded body and a top speed of 76 mph. Design features include a bar-mounted headlight and fold-down chrome rear rack headlight, plenty of underseat storage and a glove compartment.

Scooters have had a renaissance over the last few years as more commuters realize that they offer the quickest way of getting around increasingly congested cities. The updated features of the Vespa make it appealing to both sexes—men love the chrome-ringed instrument panel that looks like it belongs to an Italian sports car, while women wax lyrical about the "curry rack" which is designed for hanging small shopping bags or handbags.

LAMBRETTA LD150

Where? Various specialist vintage dealers, including www.supersonicscooters.com • www.scootermaniac.org • www.classicbikes4sale.com

How much? Around $3,000

Lambretta was the main competition for Vepsa in the 1950s and 1960s. This model has two separate seats and is capable of 52mph (84km/h). It is still popular, although production ceased in the 1970s.

Skis

K2

Where?
Ski shops • www.k2skis.com
How much?
From $450 without bindings

K2 Apache skis

Rock paintings depict hunters skiing over 5,000 years ago and the Swedish army trained on skis in the 18th century, but the first skis resembling those we know today were invented in Norway in the 19th century. In 1928, the first aluminium ski was produced in France. Today, skis are shorter, wider, and curvier than ever, with a greater variety of styles for varying levels of skill, though it's important you pick skis and have bindings adjusted to suit your ability and terrain, whether you're off for a week of trail skiing or a season of extreme endeavour. When it comes to skis, size and shape count. While jackets and goggles are all of vital importance, the true skier knows that a good-quality pair of skis is paramount. It's not about simply buying the most expensive pair, but the ones that best suit your requirements. K2 is a fine Canadian brand that has devised skis for the expert skier. The Apache group provides particularly impressive specimens that can be used in any conditions and on any terrain, due to their expert construction from a material called Titan Metal Laminate.

VOLKL

Where? www.volkl.com
How much? From $600
This German brand offers a wide selection of skis, including the Unlimited line, which can be adapted to every ski style and level. In other words, this is a great all-rounder. Volkl's skis are also equipped with "Double Grip" LT design, and a corresponding absorption system.

ROSSIGNOL

Where? Ski shops • www.rossignol.com
How much? From $300
An excellent brand with a wide range of skis, particularly for women. The Bandit B4 is good for free-riding while the Open is excellent for those one-week-a-year skiers who want control and carving power.